Understanding Today's Catholic PARISH

William J. Rademacher

■ ■ ■

John S. Weber

■ ■ ■

David McNeill, Jr.

TWENTY THIRD *23rd*

PUBLICATIONS

Twenty-Third Publications
A Division of Bayard
One Montauk Avenue, Suite 200
New London, CT 06320
(860) 437-3012 or (800) 321-0411
www.23rdpublications.com

ISBN 978-1-58595-630-2
Library of Congress Catalog Card Number: 2007930538
Printed in the U.S.A.

Contents

Foreword

A book like this should have been written a long time ago. It brings togeth-er the ecclesiology of Vatican Council II, the revised 1983 edition of the Code of Canon Law, and United States Civil Law. Rather than being an academic exercise, this volume presents these three aspects of parish life from a pastoral perspective; it does so in a way that will answer basic ques-tions when practical matters of law, canon and civil, arise in a parochial or diocesan setting.

The authors, Dr. William J. Rademacher, Rev. John Weber, JCL, and Deacon David McNeill, Esq., are well qualified to write the three sections on the parish of Vatican II, canon law and civil law, and how the three are interrelated. Dr. Rademacher has written books on the contemporary parish and has focused on parish consultative bodies. Father Weber is judi-cial vicar for the Diocese of Las Cruces, and Deacon McNeill is a practic-ing civil attorney and serves as deacon in a university parish.

The parish is where church happens. For most Catholics the parish is the place where they experience and help create the existential church. It is the parish that gives flesh and meaning to the concept of church. Moreover, it is at the parish where Catholics experience the application of church law. The sacramental life of the parish is given order, to a large degree, through the legal system of the church. The governance and administration of the parish is ordered through church law as well. Canon law establishes the way the parish is related to the bishop, the diocese, and the universal church. It also establishes the rights, privileges, and responsibilities of the pastor, as well as those of parishioners. Church law spells out procedures to be followed in various circumstances.

The Code of Canon Law requires that certain consultative structures, such as the presbyteral council (canon 495), a college of consultors (canon 502), and diocesan and parish finance councils (canons 492, 537), be established in each diocese to assist the bishop in governing the diocese and in his pastoral ministry. It is left to the bishop to establish other structures, such as diocesan synods (canons 460–68) and parish pastoral councils (canon 511).

A good example of the interaction of canon law and the parish is the parish visit by the local bishop. This visit is an opportunity for the faithful to voice their views with their bishop. As Sister Sharon Euart, RSM, explained in her talk to the Canon Law Society of Great Britain and Ireland, "Consultation in the church is rooted in the theological principles that the church is the people of God, a people gathered around their bishop, a holy people incorporated into the body of Christ with a share in the threefold mission of Christ to teach, to sanctify, and to govern" (*Origins*, vol. 35, no. 2).

The ecclesial intent for these consultative structures is for unity, that is, *communio*, in the church. In his letter *Novo Millennio Ineunte*, Pope John Paul II, urging greater communion at all levels in the church, states that "the structures of participation envisaged by Canon Law such as the priests' council and the pastoral council must be ever more highly valued" (no. 45). He went on to say that they are no less meaningful and relevant simply because they are consultative rather than deliberative. He recalls the ancient pastoral wisdom that "encouraged pastors to listen more widely to the entire people of God" (no. 45).

In the United States the need to follow the dictates of canon law on consultative structures is seen as imperative because of the clergy sexual abuse crisis of recent years. The demand for accountability and transparency in the church on behalf of the laity are joined to that of participation. The faithful rightly insist on knowing, through diocesan finance councils, of settlements made for cases of sexual abuse of minors by the clergy. The faithful want to participate, through diocesan pastoral councils and review boards, in the crafting of sexual abuse policies and procedures. Clergy personnel boards need to be informed about clergy accused of sexual abuse. Diocesan consultative structures and processes will enhance the entire church if their procedures are more widely known, their membership more representative of a wide spectrum of the diocese, and bishops and pastors made more accountable to the faithful.

The clergy sexual abuse crisis has also made us see the absolute need to be versed as much as possible on civil law as it impacts the church. The onslaught of lawsuits brought on by sexual abuse of minors has made it clearer than ever that the parish and the diocese are subject to civil law as well as to canon law. Priests study canon law in the seminary; perhaps we should study civil law as well, especially in a society where litigation is often used to settle claims. In this book the section by David McNeill on civil law is a good introduction for those of us who were taught nothing about civil law. Knowing more about civil law issues, besides what we observe on television and films, is reassuring. Civil law is not meant to be used to prey on people or institutions, nor primarily to threaten or wield punishment. It is mainly meant to protect and defend rights.

The study and knowledge of civil law on the part of church personnel will be more urgent in the future. Mark Chopko, the General Counsel of the United States Conference of Catholic Bishops, holds that in the U.S. the tenor of dialogue between church and state has changed in an unhealthy way. In a talk to the U.S. bishops in 2003, he said, "Religious institutions in this society have increasingly been subjected to pressures to conform to the culture in ways that are contrary to their teachings....Unless checked, they raise [the question] whether we will be allowed to be religiously distinct and still serve in the public arena, and even whether our internal policies and practices will be allowed to reflect church teaching." Our Catholic institutions are being pressured by placing conditions on our participation in government and even church-funded programs. There is also pressure to condition tax exemption on a willingness to abide by standards or policies that violate our teaching, such as the pressure to provide abortion services.

This book is a reminder that those of us who do the work of the church today are called to a heightened knowledge of canon and civil law. This will enable us not so much to exercise authority over others, but to serve our people with more watchful eyes and with a clearer focus on our mission to preserve our Catholic integrity and identity.

Bishop Ricardo Ramirez, CSB
Diocese of Las Cruces
September 19, 2006

Preface

"Divine Spirit...renew your wonders in our time, as though for a new Pentecost..." (Pope John XXIII convoking the Second Vatican Council, December 25, 1961).

Sister Joan Chittister, a noted author and columnist, presents a list of challenging questions in a recent column. Her questions deal with today's burning issues that cause deep concern for many Catholics: the war in Iraq, refusing communion to pro-choice politicians, the torture of prisoners, politicians who personally consider abortion immoral but support it anyway "because it's the law." On these and many other public issues there is no clear Catholic leadership. "From where I stand," Chittister concludes, "it seems to me that we are deeply confused." And Peter Steinfels, another well-known Catholic author and columnist, feels that "U.S. Roman Catholics are a people adrift." It seems clear now that U.S. parishes must themselves take on a greater leadership role.

Many Catholics have a heavy emotional investment in their parishes. After all, they celebrate the mysteries of saving grace in their parishes. With the Holy Spirit so active in our parishes, it's understandable that our parish, like the church itself, is a mystery. But it's a mystery, like Christ himself, enfleshed in the human. Thus, it's a body that lives and breathes in and through our human history. And we are that body! Sometimes we sing a joyous alleluia; other times we cry our way through a heart-rending crisis. But through it all, our church, our body, continues to grow through Pentecosts of renewal such as the Second Vatican Council. But like all humans, it also endures painful deaths in the aging parts of its body. It witnesses daily to the dying and rising of the Lord.

Our church presently is blessed with a new birth of the wonderful gifts of many lay ministers. But this means our church has to die to some of the old ways of parish life. While our church joyfully welcomes the new, it also feels the pain of dying to the old. It all adds up to a crisis of transition.

This transition is too complicated to describe in detail here. But Catholics are still dealing with the effects of the sexual abuse crisis. As a result, the moral authority of the hierarchy has diminished considerably. At the same time, our culture, including the body of the church, is moving rapidly into the age of postmodernity, which includes the rejection of authoritarian religion. Then, too, in the growing stew of determined right-wing churches, it's harder and harder for U.S. Catholics to keep their bearings. In the public square these churches are known more for what they are against (abortion, stem cell research, gay marriage) than for what they are for. And here they are getting close to the fundamentalists. All this means that our parishes cannot remain in a "drifting" mode. They have to get a new grip on their parish community's identity as they relate to the rapidly changing world around them. Otherwise, they risk falling into irrelevance or fundamentalism.

We believe *Understanding Today's Catholic Parish* will help new laborers in the vineyard define their ministries in relation to today's parish and tomorrow's world during a time of difficult transition. More and more new lay ministers are working full-time. However, we also feel this book will be especially helpful to the growing number of volunteer ministers serving on parish pastoral councils, finance councils, and so on. All in all, we hope our book will bring about a eucharistic unity among all the ministers in our rapidly changing parishes.

To become more specific, we hope the first section on pastoral theology will provide the basics for a new orientation toward our common goal. As times change, we need to reflect prayerfully on our history, identity, and mission. At the same time, in our wounded world, we need to focus our energies more deliberately on the fulfillment of our dream—the building of the kingdom of God. To do this we need a common vision for parish planning.

The second section, on canon law, is designed to bring into parish life some of the more important laws of the universal church laws that bear the wisdom of centuries. These laws also serve as one of many unifying links to the world church, which is, in turn, a life-giving part of our parish identity. All those who minister in the parish need to be familiar with the basic laws governing parish life. Ignoring these fundamental laws of governance has caused many problems in the past.

John S. Weber, the author of the canon law section, is grateful to Irene Valles and Dorothy Medina, who took over much of his work in the diocesan marriage tribunal to enable him to devote more time to work on Part II.

The parish, along with other institutions, takes its place within the larger society: the country, state, county, and city. As such, it must live and conduct its "business" within the rules of this larger society. The sexual abuse crisis, noted above, and the consequent bankruptcy of several dioceses alert all of us to the importance of our civil laws. For this reason, attorney Rev. Mr. David McNeill, Jr., has added Part III, dealing with the main civil laws affecting parish life. While the laws of these two communities, parish and state, normally do not clash, parishes simply cannot afford to live in ignorance of the laws of either community. At the same time, they need to remember that neither church nor civil laws are absolute. God's laws trump both.

David McNeill, Jr., is deeply grateful for all the help and support his wife, Francine, provided toward the completion of his section. She read his entire text and offered numerous helpful suggestions.

Finally, William J. Rademacher expresses gratitude to his wife, Elida, for her continued support while he was "married" to his computer working on Part I. He also thanks J. David McNamara and Richard Petrillo, both very busy diocesan ministers in the Las Cruces Pastoral Center. They proofread his chapters and offered many suggestions to clarify obscure passages and improve the style for easier reading.

The three of us are deeply grateful to our bishop, Ricardo Ramirez, CSB, for taking time out from his busy schedule to write the Foreword.

We now present our text to the Catholic public with the hope and prayer that, with the grace of the Holy Spirit, it will be our blessing for all ministers building up today's church.

Easter 2007
Las Cruces, New Mexico

PART I

A Pastoral Theology of the Parish

William J. Rademacher

Introduction

Since the close of Vatican II there has been a steady stream of books and articles dealing with the Catholic parish. That should not surprise us. After all, we first meet saving grace at the level of our parish. That's where, through our baptism, we first receive divine life, and where we receive a renewal of that life in our First Holy Communion and confirmation. It's where we receive forgiveness of our sins in the sacrament of reconciliation. We make our vows, "until death do us part" in our spiritual home, our parish. Finally, at the end of our earthly journey we are carried to our parish church for the Rite of Christian Burial. All this means that we have a heavy emotional and spiritual investment in our parishes. It's the basic ecclesial unit in the Catholic church.

But as an institution, the parish has come under increasing criticism since Vatican II. Bishop Ottenweller, formerly of Steubenville, Ohio, called for a total restructuring of parishes because "they are not doing their job." John Foster, in his book *Requiem for a Parish*, says the parish in its present form has "had its day."

Along with many bishops and theologians, the late Rev. Philip J. Murnion, then director of the Pastoral Life Center in New York City, made his own contributions to the stream of articles on the parish. Writing in *Origins* some years ago he described some of the weaknesses in the modern parish:

> First, is the tendency to develop ministry in terms of its existing structures, rather than to develop ministerial structures around existing needs. A second weakness is the tendency in the parish for large numbers of people to be rather anonymous and not to have the opportunity for a more personal, communal relationship in the context of which they can deepen their faith and reflect on their lives....A final weakness of the parish is the tendency of the parish's view of life to be restricted to its borders.[1]

---

1. "The Complex Task of the Parish," *Origins*, vol. 8, no. 28, 438.

The goal of the first five chapters of this book is to deal, at least to some extent, with the weaknesses listed above by Rev. Murnion. If the parish is going to develop new ministerial structures, it first needs to reflect on its own history, identity, and mission. It also needs to have the capacity to dream and have a vision of its own future. These chapters are not offered as a sacred blueprint, but are designed to stimulate debate and discussion among the people of God in their respective parishes. If these chapters activate the gift of wisdom given to all the baptized in the parish (1 Cor 12:8), they will serve a useful purpose in the upbuilding of the church and the kingdom of God.

The hope is that Part I will be especially useful to all parish ministers, parish pastoral councils, finance councils, and lay ministry students preparing to serve in the parishes and dioceses. Chapter 5: "A Vision for Parish Planning" simply represents one man's dream. My desire is that parishioners can lean on some of these ideas to push the frontiers of their own Catholic imaginations and energize their own creative talents. Thus they will come up with their own dreams for the future of their own parish. The Holy Spirit will inspire and guide their dreams and their creativity. And then there will be "the rush of a violent wind" and "tongues of fire" in every U.S. parish (Acts 2:2–3). A New Pentecost!

CHAPTER 1

A History of the Catholic Parish before Vatican Council II

Jesus did not start the Catholic parish. That much we know. So when and how did the Catholic parish come to be? To find out, we have to go back to the beginning and do a quick "rewind" of about twenty centuries of church history. It's an exciting film. It shows the power of the Spirit mightily at work in our church. At the same time, it reveals the creativity of the Christian communities across a wide variety of cultures.

The Catholic parish begins to emerge soon after Jesus ascends into heaven. The Lord's disciples gather for song, prayer, and the breaking of the bread. In its basic outline, the Christian community is shaped first by the faith of the believers who hear and respond to the Lord's word, and second by the historical and cultural conditions in which these first believers live. That's where our story begins.[1]

"Parish" in the Bible

The word "parish" comes from the Greek verb *paroikeo* meaning "to dwell by, beside, or near; to dwell as a stranger or alien without citizenship." It refers to the people's temporary sojourn in this life. This verb is used sixty times in the Septuagint version of the Old Testament.

---

1. This chapter, with minor revisions, was first published in my book *Answers for Parish Councillors* (Mystic, CT: Twenty-Third Publications, 1981).

In the Old Testament period, the noun *paroikia* (parish) means "the exile or sojourner in a strange land without citizenship or right of domicile...as opposed to the home country."[2] The noun *paroikos* (sojourner), which is used forty times in the Old Testament, refers to "the immigrant, the alien, the exile." Thus, Abraham is a *paroikos* or foreigner in Egypt (Gen 17:10); Lot is a *paroikos* in Sodom (Gen 19:9); Isaac is a *paroikos* in Canaan.

While the word *paroikia* is Greek, part of its religious meaning comes out of the faith experience of the Hebrew community. God called Abraham, demanding a total uprooting from the land where he lived. He asked Abraham to go to a foreign land to become the father of innumerable descendants. These descendants would become a community because they would be united by a threefold bond: the call, the promise, and the covenant. But Abraham and his people would always remain foreign dwellers. They would form a parish (*paroikia*), that is to say, a community of pilgrims living in an alien land. "To form part of this Hebrew community of foreigners, it was necessary to join the covenant through faith."[3] It was a covenant made on the people's side by transients, not land-owners. Thus faith, not land, united the covenanted community.

The Israelites formed a real parish community in Egypt. While living as slaves in the midst of a pagan people, they nevertheless remained faithful to the covenant, determined to continue their pilgrimage to the Promised Land.[4]

"Parish" acquired another part of its religious meaning from the Hebrew understanding of assembly (in Hebrew, *qahal*; in Greek, *ekklesia*). In the Old Testament, this assembly is the result of four distinct activities: first, the assembly is called together by the supreme authority of the people in the name of God; second, the assembly listens to the word of God and an explanation of it; third, the assembly responds to the word of God by some religious action (a sacrificial rite, a blessing, or a thanksgiving); fourth, the assembly is dismissed by the presiding official.[5]

---

2. Alex Blochlinger, *The Modern Parish Community* (New York: P.J. Kenedy and Sons, 1965), 22.

3. Casiano Floristan, *The Parish, Eucharistic Community*, John Byrne, trans. (Notre Dame, IN: Fides, 1964), 19.

4. Floristan, 19.

5. Floristan, 21.

In the New Testament, "parish" (or its derivatives) is rarely used (Lk 24:18; Heb 11:9, Acts 7:6, 29; Eph 2:19; 1 Pet 2:11; Acts 13:17; 1 Pet 1:17). However, when it is used, it retains its Old Testament meaning of aliens dwelling in a foreign land. In addition, it acquires a more mystical meaning. "The Christians know that their lives in this world are only of a temporary nature. Their real fatherland for which they were born is heaven. They are on this earth as pilgrims."[6]

In the New Testament, "church" (*ekklesia*, an assembly) and "parish" (*paroikia*, a sojourn) have, for all practical purposes, the same meaning. Since the early Christian communities are awaiting the imminent return of their Lord, they think of themselves as pilgrims or sojourners without a permanent homeland here on earth; that is, they see themselves as a *paroikia* (a parish).

In the New Testament, therefore, the parish is not a community of neighbors who live around a fixed place of worship; nor is it a territorial district. Rather, it is a community of faith living as a stranger and pilgrim in this world.

The faith of the community is more important than the place where it assembles. Nevertheless, the place of the assembly gives us some insight into the community's self-understanding. The Jerusalem community, for instance, gathers for prayer and word services in three different places: in the temple (Acts 2:4), indicating considerable continuity with Israel; in one house after the other, for the breaking of the bread; and on the porch of Solomon's temple (Acts 5:12).

No matter where it assembles, the New Testament community has a threefold mission: preaching, worship, and pastoral care. The apostles have an important role in the preaching mission (Acts 6:2-4). In the Pauline communities, however, *all* the members share some responsibility for proclaiming the word. Thus, we read in 1 Corinthians 14:26: "When you come together, each one has a hymn, a lesson, a revelation, a tongue, or an interpretation. Let all things be done for building up."

Besides the celebration of the Eucharist, the community's worship consists of baptism, imposition of hands (Acts 8:17-19), and singing of psalms, hymns, and spiritual songs (Eph 5:19-21). Pastoral care is mod-

---

6. Blochinger, 23.

eled on the image of the Good Shepherd and the service of slaves (*douloi*). The ministries of pastoral care range from the ministry of the word to the ministry of temporal administration and waiting on tables. The Christian community is formed by its song, its mission, and its celebrations.

In the New Testament, the church refers to itself both as *paroikia* (parish) and as *ekklesia* (church). When it is looking at itself in relation to this earth, as a pilgrim passing through, it refers to itself as *paroikia*. When it is looking at itself in its relation to God, as fellow citizens of the saints and members of God's household, it refers to itself as *ekklesia*. Naturally, both words are used in a non-technical sense, more descriptive than definitive.

In early Christianity, there is no established pattern of church organization. The first Christian communities are formed in the major cities (Jerusalem, Antioch, Corinth, Ephesus). Initially, a small community of families gathers in one house for word and prayer services. Such "house-churches" can hold little more than sixty people.[7] These house-churches continue until the first half of the third century. In the pastoral letters, Paul insists that church leaders be distinguished by their virtue of hospitality (1 Tim 3:2, Titus 1:7–9). No doubt, they are expected to offer their houses as places for Christian worship. Since the first Christians were Jews they also assembled in their synagogues. On their missionary journeys Paul and Barnabas routinely enter the synagogues to preach the word of God (Acts 13).

In terms of church organization, Jean Colson distinguishes two main lines of development. The first is Paul's line, which has a college of presbyters (elders) but no bishop or president. Unity is based not on a single leader, but on the theology of the body of Christ with many members and many distinct functions. These presbyterial communities (no bishop) survived long into post-apostolic times, especially in Alexandria, Egypt.

The second form of community organization is characterized by a single leader, a monarchic bishop (literally, an overseer) who resides in the community. This leader is the living image of the unity of the community.

After the apostolic period, this monarchical community (one bishop) emerges as the dominant form of church organization. Ignatius of Antioch (c. 107) leans heavily on this monarchic model to protect his flock from the

---

7. Jean-Paul Audet, *Structures of Christian Priesthood* (New York: Macmillan, 1968), 97.

triple threat posed by the Gnostics, Docetists, and conservative Jews. And it works; it protects his flock from "heresy." But, as is the case in Antioch, the gradual dominance of monarchic, or episcopal, communities is primarily the result of the church's response to specific historical situations; it is not the result or application of a set body of doctrine regarding church organization.

Episcopal Communities

From Ignatius of Antioch to the Council of Nicaea in 325, the local church is shaped by the twofold dynamic of ministry and geography. In the cities, the bishop is, at first, the ordinary pastor of the community. He presides over the Eucharist and administers the sacraments. *Parish* priests don't exist. However, the city bishop has priests, deacons, and deaconesses around him to assist him in his pastoral and charitable work. In the second and third centuries, the city is divided into regions which are placed under a deacon or priest who remains subject to the bishop. These regions are not parishes because the city bishop is still the direct superior of the entire district.

Until the Council of Nicaea there is no evidence that territory is a principle of church organization. In the cities the dominant model of church organization is that of a pastor-bishop surrounded by deacons and presbyters who go out from the bishop's altar to minister to the outlying districts of the city.

As the church spreads from the city into the country, presbyters are sent out into the surrounding villages. Very soon, however, these rural villages are cared for by *rural* bishops (*chorepiscopoi*). At first, these rural bishops are equal to the city bishops. But gradually the rural bishops become subject to the city bishops. They may not ordain priests without the permission of the city bishop. Rural bishops become very numerous. In the West, especially in Africa, bishops are appointed to every hamlet and village. "In 397 Aurelius, Bishop of Carthage, had an episcopal consecration almost every Sunday."[8] In the East, rural bishops are also very numerous. The canons specify "that a community must number at least twelve Christian males before a bishop could be elected."[9]

---

8. Blochinger, 44.

9. Blochinger, 43, note.

After Constantine (d. 337), these numerous rural bishops begin to yield to the itinerant bishops who represent the city bishops. These rural bishops are poorly educated and, therefore, susceptible to heresy and schism. Gradually, rural bishops begin to fade out of the picture. Priests begin to replace them in taking care of the pastoral work. Pope Leo I (440–61) forbids the installation of bishops in small villages and demands that the people be satisfied with a simple priest. From now on, priests in growing numbers become responsible for the rural villages.

Priests also become responsible for the titular churches, which originally are house-churches with private, secular owners. The church gradually acquires these house-churches and equips them with baptistries. Naturally, these communities are very small. Administered by married priests, these house-churches generally remain in the priest's family through inheritance from one generation of priests to the next.

Before the Council of Nicaea, both in the East and in the West, the development of the "parish" is uneven and extremely complex. Just about every principle of church organization has numerous exceptions. Since before Constantine, the church doesn't own property (again, there are exceptions), its methods of organization are almost infinitely flexible, constantly adapting to existing needs and structures. In general, church organization is determined more by sociological and political circumstances (the synagogue, trade routes, Graeco-Roman culture) than by theological or doctrinal considerations.

Within this incredible variety of church organization, only three principles emerge with any consistency. First, territory or property with boundaries is not the determining factor in defining the local church. Second, the rural priest always remains the delegate of the city bishop. He comes from the bishop's altar and is responsible to him. This remains true even when priests are appointed to regions of the city. Third, the priest does not ordain other priests. In the Western church, he does not perform the chrismation (the anointing with chrism) even when, in the absence of the bishop, he begins to administer baptism. Thus, chrismation, or confirmation, is gradually separated from baptism.

"Parish" after Constantine

In 294, the emperor Diocletian divided the Roman Empire into regional districts called "dioceses." After Constantine, the church adopted this Roman system and organized itself along the lines of the Roman diocese. In this way, the territory governed by a Roman civil magistrate is also governed by a church magistrate, such as the bishop. This is not a sudden development. In some areas, "parish" and "diocese" are used for the same district. The bishop, however, becomes the sole lawgiver and the administrator of all church property. The clergy remain under the bishop, pastorally, personally, and economically. Also, after Constantine, the churches begin to own property in their own names. The diocese becomes a juridical person under Roman law. Gradually, individual churches become juridical persons as well, and they too acquire property in their own name.

With their new freedom guaranteed by the Edict of Milan (313), Christians built oratories, churches, and monasteries at an enormous rate. Often, they are built on the graves of saints, reflecting the growing cult of the dead, which is especially evident in the rural communities.

Baptismal Churches

In the fifth century, two types of parishes develop, especially in Gaul and Spain. First in importance are the baptismal churches. These have a baptismal font, and baptism is regularly celebrated there. The second type of church, located in the smaller villages, has no baptismal font. It is dependent on the baptismal churches.

The bishop soon begins to appoint the resident archpriests to the baptismal churches. In the sixth century, he gives the archpriest the right to baptize and preach, a right that formerly was reserved to the bishop. In the ninth century, the archpriest receives the right to conduct funerals. Numerous clergy begin to gather around the baptismal churches. Often they live in community. Their wives live separately with the servants.

Privately-Owned Churches

In the eighth century, baptismal churches are gradually replaced by privately-owned churches. Such churches are often the property of families or individual laypersons. The layperson is the landlord of the church. He can sell, bequeath, or give it away. From his income, he has to maintain the priest and pay for the upkeep of the church. He can keep whatever money is left. Privately-owned churches are among the most advantageous capital investments of the period. In 826, two Roman synods, a deliberative gathering of church leaders, give papal approval to the system of privately-owned churches. This system lasts from the middle of the seventh century until the end of the ninth century. The custom of the priest expecting a fee for the administration of the sacraments originates with the privately-owned churches. In some cases, the fee is the priest's only means of support.

In the ninth and tenth centuries, this system of privately-owned churches declines as a result of numerous abuses, which reduces the management of church property to a lucrative trade. The Gregorian Reform, which culminated in the First and Second Lateran Councils (1123 and 1139), reserves to bishops alone the right to appoint priests to churches. Lay ownership of churches is now forbidden. The decrees of these Lateran Councils are so rigorously enforced that privately-owned churches cease to exist by the end of the twelfth century.

The Benefice System

A benefice, in its developed form, can be defined as a legal right permanently constituted by a competent ecclesiastical authority and consisting of a sacred office and the right to receive the revenue accruing from the endowment of that office.

From the tenth century to the Council of Trent (1545–63), the parish is shaped by the acceptance of the benefice system, by the adoption of the tithe as a system of support, by the building of parish schools, by lay involvement in temporal administration, and by an increase in social activities centered around the parish. The benefice system actually begins to evolve in the sixth century; however, it is not adopted by the universal church until the eleventh.

A benefice has four main characteristics: 1) perpetuity; 2) the right to revenue from church property; 3) a formal decree of ecclesiastical authority giving to certain funds or property the title of a benefice; 4) an annexed office of spiritual functions, such as the care of souls or the exercise of jurisdiction.

What is important about a benefice is the endowment that goes with it. This consists of the goods owned by the benefice, the obligatory payments of a family, the voluntary offerings of the faithful, and the fees payable to the priest who holds the office attached to the benefice.

Important, too, is the fact that a benefice has an objective perpetuity. It continues to exist even after the priest who holds it is transferred or dies. It has legal existence all by itself. Thus, there arises a clear distinction between the benefice, the office, and the priest. Also, property or endowment now becomes an important element in the identity of the parish.

In the context of the parish, the office is the position of directing and running the parish and of performing the spiritual functions required in the care of souls. The appointment to office is gradually reserved to the bishop, who can appoint an ordained or non-ordained person. In practice, he appoints an ordained priest who then gets his room and board from the revenues of the benefice.

The adoption of the tithe as a system of church support requires members of the parish to contribute ten percent of their income in produce or grain to their parish. It has its origin in the Old Testament Mosaic Law. As early as 585, the tithe becomes obligatory, both by civil and by ecclesiastical law (under pain of excommunication). The practical effect of the tithe is to tie parishioners more closely to a particular parish. They rightly expect sacramental services from the parish that receives their tithe. In the absence of any territorial principle, the tithe becomes the bond of belonging.

In 845, some parishes begin to build schools. "Bishop Hincmar of Rheims expresses his desire to build a school in every parish."[10] At this time, too, the church becomes the center for social and business activities: "purchase of gifts and all public acts took place there. Slaves were freed before the altar. The church served as archive, and often enough in the country, as a barn or threshing floor. It provided sanctuary for fugitives, but was also used for legal processes, banquets, plays, and dancing."[11]

In thirteenth-century Germany, laypersons have the right to vote in selecting their own parish priest. They have presentation and nomination rights. In France, it is common practice for laypersons to be responsible for the temporal administration of the parish.

---

10. Blochinger, 75.
11. Blochinger, 75.

Throughout the Middle Ages, the civil and parish communities are basically one and the same. Serving both ecclesial and secular interests, it is at the same time church and civic community.

The Council of Trent

The parish as we know it today was basically shaped during and after the Council of Trent (1545–63). Now the parish priest alone becomes responsible for the care of souls. The faithful of the diocese are divided into clearly defined parishes, each served by its own parish priest. The council deals with the problem of the parish in its twenty-fourth session:

> In those cities and localities where the parochial churches have no definite boundaries, and whose rectors have not their own people whom they may rule but administer the sacraments indiscriminately to all who desire them, the holy council commands the bishops that, for the greater security of the salvation of the souls committed to them, they divide the people into definite and distinct parishes and assign to each its own permanent parish priest, who can know his people and from whom alone they may licitly receive the sacraments; or that they make other, more beneficial provisions as the conditions of the locality require. They shall also see to it that the same is done as soon as possible in those cities and localities where there are no parish churches; any privileges and customs whatsoever, even though immemorial, notwithstanding.[12]

After Trent, the territorial principle, with clearly established boundaries, becomes the norm for establishing parishes. There are some exceptions; the *personal* principle is used to establish special parishes for those who belong to different rites and for those who belong to national minorities, such as Polish, Slovak, Italian, and the like.

Yet, it is mainly the parishioners living within clearly defined boundaries who constitute the average parish. Even though, in principle, each parish is supposed to have its own church, Rome does, by way of exception, allow several parishes to use the same church.

---

12. As quoted in Sabbas J. Kilian, OFM, *Theological Models for the Parish* (New York: Alba House, 1977), 6.

With the Council of Trent, the division and establishment of new parishes is reserved to the bishop. After him, the parish priest has exclusive authority over the parishioners. He receives the right to baptize and to anoint the sick. He is charged with the duty to preach on Sundays and during Lent and Advent. He must from now on keep a register of all baptisms and marriages. Lay Christians now become passive subordinates who are subject to the pastor. According to the more rigid theologians, their main duty is obedience.

After Trent, authority becomes concentrated in the bishop and his delegate, the pastor. Where there is a parish school, the pastor becomes responsible for running the school and for hiring and firing the teachers.

Parishes grow larger. By the end of the nineteenth century, the parishes in Paris average 36,000 people. In many French parishes, it is physically impossible for all parishioners to fulfill their Easter duty. In Germany, conditions are the same. In South America they are worse, with an average of 50,000 "members" per parish.

In the United States, the church sets up its parishes according to the European model, as directed by the Council of Trent. It relies primarily on the territorial principle for parish organization. Of course, there are numerous exceptions for national or personal parishes for the growing number of immigrants who speak a common language.

Lay Trusteeism

Toward the end of the eighteenth century and through much of the nineteenth, the church in the United States had to deal with lay trusteeism (1785–1884). The *Catholic Encyclopedia* defines trusteeism as "a form of insubordination in which lay parishioners, particularly lay parish trustees, on the basis of civil law, claimed excessive parochial administrative powers, and even the right to choose and dismiss pastors."

The reason for adopting the trustee system in the United States is clearly stated by Vincent Harold, OP, in his letter to Rome:

> Each church is, by an act of legislature of the state in which it is situated, made a distinct corporation, and this incorporated body possesses all the rights and privileges of a citizen of the States....The income of the churches is principally derived from an annual rent which each member of the congregation pays for

his seat (pew) in the church....These pew rents and burial charges are recoverable by law. It was considered an odious and a dangerous thing for the priest to appear in a Court of Justice, as the prosecutor of his flock even for the recovery of just debts. Yet this would sometimes have been inevitable had he been appointed the legal representative of the church property. It was therefore thought prudent that a certain number of the respectable lay members of each church should be elected for these purposes. The pastor is always President of the Board, and no act of the trustees can have legal force without his signature. To prevent the abuse of power the lay trustees are annually elected. The priest is the only member whom the law recognizes as permanent without election.[13]

Trusteeism had some European roots in the church wardens of Germany and France. It becomes a problem in the U.S. church between 1785 and 1884. It is largely confined to New York, Pennsylvania, and Louisiana. The problem develops from a combination of factors: unruly priests, "old world" nationalist feelings, poor education of the laity, and appeals to civil law to solve property disputes.

The difficulties of the trustee system are often exaggerated by clerical historians who see the problem as a threat to the pyramid of their authority. Leonard Swidler writes: "In the three quarters of a century of controversy over the trustee system there do not seem to have been much more than a dozen prominent trustee difficulties in all the United States...."[14]

Bishop John Carroll (1736–1815) had defended the trustee system, including the right of the laity to have a voice in the appointment of pastors: "Wherever parishes are established no doubt a proper regard (and such is suitable to our government) will be had to rights of the congregation in the mode of election and representation."[15]

In 1829, the First Council of Baltimore effectively eliminated the problem of lay trusteeism. It ruled that, wherever possible, no church is to be

---

13. As cited in Leonard Swidler, "People, Priests, and Bishops in U.S. Catholic History," *Bishops and People* (Philadelphia: Westminster Press, 1970), 117–18.

14. Swidler, 118.

15. Swidler, 120.

erected without being legally assigned to the bishop.[16] After this council, the bishops and priests adopt a more clerical and authoritarian style of parish administration, a style that is largely supported by the peasant and conservative immigrants who pour into the United States at this time. Because of the difficulties with trusteeism, American parishes come more and more under the control of the bishop. They also move further away from the congregationalism of their Protestant neighbors.

The Code of Canon Law

The Code of Canon Law was published in 1917. The canons on the parish basically repeat the parochial principle as laid down by the Council of Trent in 1563. Canon 216, no. 1, states: "The territory of every diocese is to be divided into distinct territorial parts; to each part is to be assigned its own church with a definite part of the population, and its own rector as the proper pastor of that territory is to be put in charge for the necessary care of souls." Canon 451 lays down the principle that the pastor remains dependent on the bishop. He is responsible "for the care of souls under the authority of his bishop."

Since the publication of the 1917 Code of Canon Law, a parish is understood as "a distinct, clearly limited territory and distinct, clearly determined population with its own proper church and its own proper pastor."[17] Many commentators note that canon law does not define, but merely describes, the parish. At least one theologian points out that the parish of the 1917 code is based on an inadequate ecclesiology, is exclusively legalistic, and one-sidedly clerical.[18]

Vatican Council II

Vatican II (1962–65) does not specifically address the theology of the parish. It follows the Council of Trent in describing the parish in a relationship of dependence between the pastor and his bishop:

16. Swidler, 122.

17. Kilian, 8.

18. Charles Davis, "The Parish and Theology," *Clergy Review*, 48 (1964), 269.

But because it is impossible for the bishop always and everywhere to preside over the whole flock in his church he cannot do other than establish lesser groupings of the faithful. Among these, parishes set up locally under a pastor *who takes the place of the bishop* are the most important: for in a certain way they represent the visible church as it is established throughout the world.[19]

In its *Decree on the Pastoral Office of Bishops in the Church*, Vatican II does, however, depart rather significantly from Trent's territorial definition of diocese when it states:

A diocese is a section of the people of God entrusted to a bishop to be guided by him with the assistance of his clergy so that loyal to its pastor and formed by him into one community in the Holy Spirit through the gospel and the Eucharist it constitutes one particular church in which the one, holy, catholic and apostolic church of Christ is truly present and active.[20]

As is evident in Vatican II's definition, the accent now is on the people of God rather than on territory. If this shift from territory to people is applied to the parish level, many new models of parish become possible. This new emphasis on the believing people will have profound effects in shaping the future theology of the modern parish.

For Reflection and Discussion

1. What surprised you the most in reading the history of the Catholic parish?

2. What parts of this history do you feel could be adopted by today's parish?

3. How do you react to the fact that in Carthage they consecrated a new bishop almost every Sunday?

4. What do you make of the fact that the Jewish synagogue was the home of the early Christian churches?

5. Have you ever wondered whether parish pastoral councils would give us the same problems as the lay trustee system? Why or why not?

---

19. Walter M. Abbott, ed., "Constitution on the Sacred Liturgy," *The Documents of Vatican II* (New York: Herder and Herder, 1966), no. 42 (italics mine).

20. Austin Flannery, ed., *Vatican Council II* (Northport, NY: Costello Publishing, 1992), no. 11.

CHAPTER 2

The U.S. Catholic Parish since Vatican Council II

The changes in the life of the U.S. parish in the last forty years have been called "amazing," "tremendous," and "revolutionary." Adjectives multiply. No doubt U.S. Catholics have experienced more changes in their parishes since the close of the Second Vatican Council (1965) than during any other period in history. Because many of these changes are still in process, it's difficult to describe a "before" and "after." Change continues, and, in some areas, at a rapid pace. Due to space limitations it's impossible to provide a detailed description of today's parish in transition. Fortunately, many competent authors have applied their scholarly talents to research the modern parish.[1] On the other hand, we can attempt a brief outline of the major forces that have impacted and changed the life of the U.S. parish since the close of the Second Vatican Council.

Renewal of the Liturgy

Perhaps the most significant change came with Vatican II's renewal of the liturgy. On the First Sunday of Advent, 1965, the centuries-old Latin Mass is

---

1. See especially: Peter Steinfels, *A People Adrift* (New York: Simon and Schuster, 2003); Jay Dolan, *In Search of an American Catholicism* (Oxford, NY: Oxford University Press, 2002); Jay Dolan, R. Scott Appleby, Patricia Byrne, and Debra Campbell, *Transforming Parish Ministry* (New York: Crossroad, 1989); Thomas Bokenkotter, *Dynamic Catholicism* (New York: Doubleday, 1992); Patricia Foster and Thomas Sweetser, *Transforming the Parish* (Franklin, WI: Sheed and Ward, 1999); and Paul Wilkes, *Excellent Catholic Parishes* (Mahwah, NJ: Paulist Press, 2001) .

suddenly replaced by a vernacular liturgy. The *Dominus vobiscum*, so familiar to Catholic ears, passes quietly into history. Now Catholics across the land move from passive spectators to active participation in the liturgy in their own language. For centuries silent in church, Catholics now begin to sing and even greet one another with the sign of peace during their Sunday liturgy.

For some Catholics the changes in church architecture that come with the liturgical renewal are shocking. Communion railings, which separated the "priest's" sanctuary from the congregation, are suddenly removed. Now the sanctuary is no longer the sacred preserve of the priest. Laypersons, including women, walk freely to the altar to help the priest as extraordinary ministers of the Eucharist. Statuary, often the object of prayerful devotion, is removed or relocated. The altar, for centuries facing the wall, is moved forward to face the people. The priest presider now faces the people while celebrating the liturgy. Many of these changes, unfortunately, are merely announced from the pulpit without first consulting or educating the parishioners. Parish pastoral councils still do not exist.

New churches often adopt semi-circular designs as opposed to the narrow "tunnel" churches of the past. The choir, formerly hidden in the loft in the back of the church, suddenly takes its place near the sanctuary. Now the choir becomes an integral part of the liturgy. The laws of fasting and abstinence for Lent and the Eucharist are modified and given a less legalistic interpretation.

The seven sacraments are also revised and changed. Now they, too, are celebrated in the people's mother tongue. Everybody can participate. Baptism is often celebrated during the Sunday liturgy so the whole parish community can share in this community event. Baptism becomes a public initiation into a faith community, rather than a mere removal of the stain of original sin. The sacrament of penance, or confession, becomes the sacrament of reconciliation, now also called a sacrament of healing. The dark confessional bins in the back or side of the church are replaced by pleasant, well-lit reconciliation chapels. Catholics now have the option of confessing privately, as in the "old days," or face to face with the priest.

The sacrament of extreme unction becomes the sacrament of the anointing of the sick. It's a liturgical and communal celebration, whether celebrated in the home, in the hospital, or in the church. In actual practice it's often celebrated in conjunction with the Sunday liturgy. It becomes a sacrament not for the dying, but for the sick. For this reason it is also called a sacrament of healing.

Devotional practices change as well. Thomas Bokenkotter, a distinguished church historian, summarizes the changes in Marian devotions:

> The impact of the Council (Vatican II) on Marian devotion has been tremendous. Devotion to Mary declined precipitously as old forms of piety disappeared with little replacement. Rosaries and scapulars were discarded, statues of Mary were removed from many parish churches, old hymns faded from memory, and May Day celebrations disappeared.[2]

The renewal of liturgical music takes on a high priority. Pastors hire full-time music directors to train both choirs and people to sing the actual texts of the vernacular liturgy. Music is no longer an "add-on" superimposed on the liturgy, but an integral part of it.

The liturgical renewal means recruiting and training lay lectors to proclaim the Scriptures. Many lay communion ministers are also needed to help distribute holy communion during the liturgy. They also take the Eucharist to the sick members of the parish in their homes or in nursing homes. Even today some older Catholics are adjusting to this new way of being church.

Relations with Other Religions

The Second Vatican Council passed its landmark *Decree on Ecumenism* on November 21, 1964. In it the bishops of the council "summon the church to a continual reformation" and beg the pardon of God and of their separated brothers and sisters for the church's "sins against unity." In response, Catholic parishes generally abandon their defensive stance against neighboring Protestant churches. Pastors even join the local ministerial associations. Their parishioners cooperate on many ecumenical projects with members of other faiths. Protestants are no longer called or thought of as heretics, but as sisters and brothers.

---

2. *Dynamic Catholicism* (New York: Doubleday, 1992), 135. See also Jay Dolan, *In Search of American Catholicism*, 238–40.

In October 1965, Vatican II approved *A Declaration on the Relationship of the Church to Non-Christian Religions*. Originally a chapter in the *Decree on Ecumenism*, it grew into a separate document. It encourages positive relationships with Buddhism, Hinduism, and the Islamic faith. It reminds Catholics that these religions "often reflect a ray of that Truth which enlightens all men." Regarding the hostilities between Christians and Muslims, it advises "all to forget the past and to strive sincerely for mutual understanding."[3] So far, U.S. Catholic parishes, in spite of this declaration, have not engaged in much ecumenical outreach to the growing numbers of Muslims in the U.S. There is little effort "to make common cause of safeguarding and fostering social justice, moral values, peace, and freedom."[4] A dialogic relationship with Muslims is long overdue. But often age-old hostilities, dating to the era of the Crusades, continue.

Church Governance

The style of governance in the parishes changes considerably with the introduction of parish pastoral councils. In the early stages, some pastors express fears of the resurgence of the lay trustee problems noted in Chapter 1. By 1995, however, seventy-nine percent of parishes have active parish pastoral councils. These councils often have a policy-making role in the governance of their parishes. While the new Code of Canon Law (1983) limits these councils to a "consultative" role, many pastors work well in a collaborative style with the lay and religious members of their councils. The pastor's veto or non-ratification of the councils' resolutions, in practice, is limited to rare moral and doctrinal issues. Some councils, on the other hand, are still suffering through their growing pains and still dependent on a specific pastor's skill and comfort with the whole consultative process. But the good news is that most pastors and councils are making the required adjustment to this new governing style. Parishes with a parish school often adopt a school board system of governance.

---

3. Walter M. Abbott, *The Documents of Vatican II* (New York: Herder and Herder, 1966), *A Declaration on the Relationship of the Church to Non-Christian Religions*, nos. 2, 3. All further quotations from Vatican II documents will be from this Abbott edition. However, the references will be to the numbers in the text, rather than to specific pages. For readers who do not have the Abbott edition, the Flannery edition keeps the same numbers.

4. Abbott, *A Declaration on the Relationship of the Church to Non-Christian Religions*, no. 4.

Role of Women in the Church

The women's movement has had a profound effect on the life of the church and the parish. It has created some tensions with the church's "patriarchal authoritarianism." Women's issues, including the ordination of women to the deaconate and priesthood, are now hotly debated at parish meetings. "Several studies conclude that Catholic women are quite angry with their church....More women feel alienated in the Catholic church than in any other denomination," noted one study.[5] Many have joined the "twenty million Catholics who do not belong to a parish."[6] "The pervasive nature of sexism in the church," said one woman, "is a burden of stone strapped to the backs of women."[7]

In spite of these tensions, a growing number of women are showing heroic love and compassion for their frail, patriarchal church. They devote themselves with zeal, competence, and dedication to a variety of full-time ministries on parish staffs and in diocesan offices. "By 1999...eighty-two percent of paid parish ministers were women."[8] These women are a great gift to the church during its growing clergy shortage. They are sacraments of saving grace where otherwise there would be a large vacuum in the church's pastoral ministry.

Birth Control Encyclical

It has been called a Catholic Vietnam, or better, a Catholic earthquake. The aftershocks have been felt throughout the Catholic world for many years, and especially at the parish level. The real shock was Pope Paul VI's encyclical *Humanae Vitae*. Published on July 29, 1968, it taught that every act of marital sexual intercourse must be open to the conception of new life. That meant a final "no" to artificial contraception of whatever kind.

The birth control question had been removed from the agenda of the Second Vatican Council. Pope John XXIII had appointed a special commission to study the birth control issue, and many Catholics, conditioned by all

---

5. Jay Dolan, *In Search of an American Catholicism*, 236.

6. Dolan, 236.

7. Dolan, 235.

8. Dolan, 229.

the changes of Vatican II, expected a change. But Pope Paul VI rejected the majority report of the papal commission and ruled in favor the traditional church teaching. The encyclical caused reverberations of seismic proportions among theologians, priests, and Catholic laity. Rev. Andrew Greeley, a well-known research scholar, feels the birth control encyclical has "canceled out the positive results of Vatican II" and caused "a catastrophic collapse of the old Catholic sexual ethic." It also caused a polarization of the church between those who are for and those who are against the encyclical.

At the level of the Catholic parish, the encyclical's teaching has been widely ignored. In this case "the body of the faithful, anointed as they are by the Holy One," may be relying on "a supernatural sense of the faith which characterizes the people as a whole...showing universal agreement in matters of faith and morals."[9] In a 1993 survey, nine out of ten Catholics agreed that "someone practicing artificial birth control can still be a good Catholic."[10] Like the former papal teaching on slavery, usury, the Copernican theory, and Galileo, this encyclical may be another case of non-reception. In the Middle ages, theology accepted "the theological principle of *non-acceptatio legis*, or the rejection of the law from above by opposition at the base."[11]

Nowadays, however, the non-acceptance of the pope's teaching has many deleterious side effects. Besides the loss of credibility in papal teaching authority, Peter Steinfels lists other harmful, long-range consequences of the birth control encyclical:

> alienating the majority of the faithful,...lowering the caliber of bishops, weakening their national conferences; crippling discussion of marriage, family life, and sexual issues generally; isolating church teaching authorities in a clerical culture; surrounding all claims about teaching authority with confusion and suspicion; stigmatizing some of the best theological scholars; and forcing priests to hide their true convictions.[12]

9. See Vatican II's *Dogmatic Constitution on the Church*, no.12.

10. Steinfels, 258.

11. Edward Schillebeeckx, "The Christian Community and Its Officebearers," *The Right of the Community to a Priest*, Edward Schillebeeckx and Johann-Baptist Metz, eds. (New York: Seabury Press, 1980), 121.

12. Steinfels, 26.1

To Steinfels's list we can add that large numbers of Catholics gave up the sacrament of reconciliation entirely. And some bishops and priests simply entered a period of silence about morality in sexual matters. This silence has been described a "paralysis of leadership" at a time when sexual values and behavior were undergoing profound changes.

However, the bishops have not really been silent. In 1980, the U.S. bishops founded the Diocesan Development Program for Natural Family Planning. It provides help to dioceses to train teachers and organize classes for couples to learn more about Natural Family Planning. This initiative gave birth to several associations and diocesan programs to encourage Natural Family Planning. Presently these programs are receiving more support than the inaccurate "calendar" or "rhythm method" that was promoted before and after *Humanae Vitae*.

Permanent Deacons

There's also good news to report during this turbulent postconciliar period. The number of permanent deacons ministering in the parishes increases daily. The *Official Catholic Directory* (2003) reports that there are 14,106 permanent deacons serving in U.S. parishes. This is a fifty percent increase in the last ten years. Permanent deacons "take their turn" preaching during the Sunday liturgy. Besides presiding at baptisms, weddings, and funerals, they conduct Sunday communion service in the absence of a priest. They routinely minister to the sick and take Viaticum to the dying. Many conduct classes to prepare people for baptism and marriage. Their specific ministries can vary considerably depending on their pastor, their age, their own gifts, and their unique experience.

The married permanent deacons bring a totally new dimension to the parish ministry. They are committed both to their church and to the world. Working daily at their secular jobs, they bridge the gap between the sacred and the secular. By their witness they teach the rest of the parish that ministry is not confined to the church or to the sanctuary.[13] Their daily workaday world brings a new interpretation to Paul's tent-making ministry. At the same time, they witness to the more positive view of the world as expressed

---

13. See Thomas Baker, "Two Cheers for Deacons," *Church* 19 (Winter 2003), 14.

in Vatican II's *Pastoral Constitution on the Church in the Modern World*.[14] They also prove that marriage is not an obstacle to a fruitful ministry. On the contrary, their supporting wives enhance their ministries. The wives confirm the wisdom of Paul's advice: "Let deacons be married only once, and let them manage their children and their households well" (1 Tim 3:12).

Lay Ministers

Perhaps the most significant change since Vatican II, especially in large parishes, is the employment of full- and part-time lay ministers, especially women, to serve on the parish staff. Many women have earned theological degrees with distinction. Lay volunteers often find themselves working not with the priest, but with full-time lay staff.

These full-time lay ministers continue to make significant changes in the U.S. parish. Already in 1984, *The Notre Dame Study of Catholic Parish Life* found that "83% of the leadership within Catholic parishes, paid or unpaid, were laypersons....Even among the paid staff...57% were lay....By 1999 as many as 29,146 lay people and religious were working as paid parish ministers in the nation's Catholic parishes."[15]

Dioceses across the country are also recognizing that all these lay ministers need special training. By 2003 a total of 35,000 laypersons were enrolled in 313 formation programs in 147 dioceses in 49 states and the District of Columbia.[16] Three types of training programs are offered: degree programs at Catholic universities, diocesan programs conducted at a central location such as a retreat house, and parish-based programs in which four or five parishes come together at a central location. Sixty percent of the total enrollment in these programs are women.[17] The National Association for Lay Ministry (NALM), based in Washington, DC, has been both a guide and an inspiration to these lay ministry training programs. Parishioners are getting used to attending parish religious services conducted by lay persons. No doubt Peter Steinfels has it right: "The

---

14. See especially Abbott, nos. 53–57.

15. Dolan, *In Search of an American Catholicism*, 229.

16. *The CARA Report*, 8 (Spring 2003), 5. This is the publication of the Center for Applied Research in the Apostolate.

17. *The CARA Report*, 7 (Spring 2002), 8.

leadership throughout American Catholicism is changing. Nothing can stop that. Leadership by priests and nuns is giving way to leadership by lay people."[18]

For many lay ministers the adjustment of the clerical structures to this new lay reality has been painfully slow. In many parishes lay ministers still do not have contracts, clear job descriptions, quarterly reviews, grievance procedures, or job security. The arrival of a new pastor may mean lay ministers find themselves out of a job. And so far, they cannot have recourse to diocesan arbitration boards, which do not exist.

Shortage of Priests

Perhaps the most serious changes in parish life are caused by the continuing shortage of priests. While in 2003 the number of Catholics in the U.S. has increased to 63,347,000, the number of priestless parishes in 2000 had increased to 3,040. In 2002, a total of 313 parishes were administered by laypersons; 114, by permanent deacons.[19] In the meantime, parishes are being closed, merged, clustered, and consolidated. Some parishes are closed due to the movement of populations; others are closed due to the growing shortage of priests. Dioceses want to ensure the celebration of the Eucharist in every parish. But this is not easy to do. The number of Catholic clergy in the U.S. declined by twenty-two percent: from 58,534 in 1981 to 45,713 in 2001.

The painful tragedy in the declining numbers of priest presiders is the gradual loss of the full Eucharist, the heart of the Catholic parish. Without a priest-presider, in the present church discipline, there can be no celebration of the full Eucharist. As the years go on, the Eucharist will no longer be central to Catholic life. The parishes continue to pray for an increase in vocations to the priesthood, but so far the decline continues. One pastor commented: "Maybe we should be praying that our bishops remove the church-created obstacles to vocations: gender and celibacy." In 2004, a total of 876 priests had signed petitions to the U.S. bishops for optional celibacy or for the ordination of married men.

---

18. Steinfels, 307.

19. *The CARA Report*, 7 (Winter 2002), 7.

The dire predictions of Forster and Sweetser (1993) are being fulfilled in our own time:

> The danger is that the shortage of ordained priests and the corresponding scarcity of the Eucharist and the sacraments will lead to a collapse of the small parish. The pressure to make the Eucharist available to all will create a new configuration of mega-parishes that offer only a few Masses that are attended by large congregations. Priesthood, in other words, is the first issue that will have to be addressed within the next ten years.[20]

With the creation of mega-parishes, Catholics are losing the sense of community many are seeking in response to our individualistic culture. The first Christian communities were indeed small bread-breaking communities gathered in private homes. In our own time, Woman Church, founded in 1983, is trying to recover a sense of the small community in its eucharistic celebrations:

> Numbers of women, both religious and lay, began to gather in informal groups to celebrate the Eucharist without including a priest as their celebrant. This is a fairly widespread phenomenon found throughout the country. One woman said: "...we gather to pray with people whom we love and know as a faith-family...."[21]

The territorial principle of parish organization, observed since the Council of Trent and still required by canon law, is often not observed in actual practice. Research on Mass attendance indicates that "twenty-five percent of Mass attendees say they usually attend a parish other than the one closest to their home." Nineteen percent simply shop for a church, choosing their parish for the sense of community or for the preaching. With our modern expressways in our large cities, street addresses and boundaries are no longer a compelling reason to choose a parish community.

Multiculturalism

The growing multiculturalism continues to shape the U.S. parish as never

---

20. *Transforming the Parish*, 206.
21. Dolan, *In Search of an American Catholicism*, 235.

before.[22] Jorge Ramos of Univision, may have it right: "The United States is not a white country; it is a multiethnic and multicultural nation. In less than sixty years it will be a nation composed solely of minorities."[23] Ramos feels the era of the melting pot is over.[24] The new immigrants, he reports, are clinging to their own languages and cultural symbols. Today, the same street will have a Mediterranean Restaurant, an Asian Nails, a Chinese Buffet, and a Mexican Tortilleria. "Nine out of every ten Hispanics speak Spanish at home,"[25] and, no doubt, on their cell phones. They watch Univision more than CNN. In the year 2000, thirty-two percent of U.S. Catholics were Hispanic. By 1990, there were seven million Asians living in the United States, and a fourth of the Archdiocese of San Francisco was Filipino.[26] But, regarding the end of the melting pot, doubts remain. Only time will tell whether the new immigrants' children can resist the powerful onslaught of the U.S. culture.

In any event, the Catholic parish is gradually adjusting to the new ethnic reality. "In Los Angeles there are seventy-two ethnic groups within the Catholic church; on any Sunday the Catholic Mass is celebrated in forty-seven languages."[27] At St. Brigid's parish in Westbury, New York, "every Sunday the Mass is celebrated in four different languages—English, Spanish, Italian, and Creole."[28]

Parishes are still learning to live with the tensions both within and between these various ethnic groups. At the same time, they need to do considerable prayerful discernment about what elements in a specific culture can be blessed and what elements need to be exorcised. In view of the enfleshment of the God-man into a specific Jewish culture, the church is ready to embrace each new culture with respect and even reverence.

---

22. See "Cultural Pluralism in the United States," *Pastoral Letters of the United States Catholic Bishops*, vol. IV (Washington, DC, 1984), 364–76.

23. *No Borders* (New York: HarperCollins, 2002), 117.

24. See Jorge Ramos, *The Latino Wave* (New York: HarperCollins, 2004), 69–107.

25. *No Borders*, 118.

26. Dolan, *In Search of an American Catholicism*, 220–21.

27. Dolan, *In Search of an American Catholicism*, 220–21.

28. Dolan, *In Search of an American Catholicism*, 222.

On the other hand, the church needs to be wary of a given culture's superstitious practices and avoid the dangers of syncretism. Not everything in either the Asian or the U.S. culture can uncritically be placed in the service of the gospel. Jesus was highly critical of certain elements in his own Jewish culture: "But woe to you Pharisees! For you...neglect justice" (Lk 11:42). Thus the tensions and challenges of inculturation remain. The church must cling to the profound meaning of the incarnation. At the same time, it cannot abandon its prophetic ministry in favor of achieving a superficial harmony in a multicultural parish community. The church's gospel always stands in critical judgment over all of the world's diverse cultures, including that of the U.S. A multicultural society, especially in the U.S., always runs the risk of becoming a religiously indifferent culture.

Social Justice

Well over one hundred years after the publication of *On the Condition of Workers* (1891), the first of six social justice encyclicals, some parishes are tip-toeing into social justice issues. With the help and encouragement of diocesan offices, parishes and their parish pastoral councils are getting involved in immigration issues, war and peace, human rights, repeal of the death penalty, domestic violence, poverty, racial discrimination, housing for the poor, ecology, Fair Trade (as opposed to Free Trade), and globalization issues.[29] Some parishes are now responding to our growing ecological crisis. No doubt parish stewardship campaigns will soon include "planetary stewardship."

But most Catholic parishes have a long way to go. They are discovering that it is easier to give bread to the poor (charity) than to ask the challenging question: "Why do the poor have no bread?" (social justice). With this last question they confront the existing social structures and the political system. In spite of numerous social encyclicals and bishops' pastoral letters, many Catholics, conditioned by the American individualistic culture, feel religion should remain a private affair. Besides that, they feel religion should

---

29. For more information on Fair Trade, see "Fair Trade Tea, Father?" *The Tablet* (March 6, 2004), 17. Joy Bosworth directs the campaign to get the parishes in the Diocese of Lancaster, England, "to serve Fair Trade products at every available opportunity." There now are over 250 products available.

remain in the sanctuary, or at least in the church. Formed by the American media, they uncritically repeat our culture's mantra: "Religion should stay out of politics." And social justice issues are almost always part of the political order. Often these issues, such as racial discrimination, are in our blood as part of our culture's pathology. Our frail faith, vulnerable in a human vessel, is not immune to our culture's social diseases. So we abandon our prophetic ministry and take refuge behind the so-called wall of the separation of the sacred and the secular. So culture conquers faith. "The salt of the earth loses its taste" (Mt 5:13). The dough transforms the yeast. Through unconscious cultural osmosis we become more American than Catholic. In many parishes Catholic social teaching still remains our best kept secret.[30]

Fortunately, competent help is available. Parishes can now subscribe to *Network Connection*, the newsletter of the National Catholic Social Justice Lobby based in Washington, DC. The Network's stated mission and vision:

> educates, lobbies, and organizes to influence the formation of federal legislation to promote economic and social justice;…envisions a social, economic, and political order that ensures human dignity and ecological justice; celebrates racial, ethnic, and cultural diversity; and promotes the common good.

The Network is especially effective in relating the papal teaching on social justice to current social problems in the United States.[31]

Sexual Abuse Crisis and Accountability

In the beginning of 2002, the U.S. Catholic parish found itself in an unprecedented crisis. The revelation in Boston of the sexual abuse of children by priests caused shock and a profound sadness among the faithful across the land. The discovery that the crime had been covered up by some U.S. bishops caused a loss of credibility in the bishops' leadership and moral authority. Many parishioners, understandably, lost faith in the church's monarchic form of government. They demanded less secrecy, less

---

30. See Michael Schultheis, Edward DeBerri, and Peter Henriot, *Our Best Kept Secret* (Washington, DC: Center of Concern, 1987).

31. To subscribe, write to: Network, 801 Pennsylvania Ave., SE, Washington, DC 20003-2167. Another resource for social justice issues is: Quixote Center, P.O. Box 5206, Hyattsville, MD 20782.

clericalism, and more public accountability from their leadership. The costs of legal and court fees have forced some dioceses into bankruptcy. It's too early, at this time, to assess the spiritual and financial impact of this scandal on the U.S. parish. No doubt there will have to be some serious changes in the form of church government, with the accent on more accountability at all levels. Mutual accountability goes to the very heart of what it means to belong to the church:

> We are mutually accountable to each other for our lives. We may still live in our private houses and have our private bank accounts, but, once we belong to a church, we no longer fully own our lives. We now have to answer to each other and may no longer claim our own lives as an exclusive piece of property.[32]

In the still unfolding crisis two hopeful signs appear on the horizon: the growth of groups like Call to Action and Voice of the Faithful and the strong possibility of a Fourth Plenary U.S. Council. Voice of the Faithful was organized in 2002 in response to the sexual abuse scandal. By the end of the year it had thirty thousand members from more than forty U.S. states and twenty-one countries. Its stated mission is "to provide a prayerful voice, attentive to the Spirit, through which the faithful can actively participate in the governance and guidance of the Catholic church."[33] Its goal is "to shape structural change within the church...to work from the parish level upward...to work vigorously for immediate, meaningful lay consultation in the process of pastoral selection."[34]

A second hopeful sign is the real prospect of a Plenary U.S. Council. In 2003, over one hundred bishops had signed a petition to convoke such a council. If such a council includes a large number of competent lay participants, it could address the crisis in church governance with the totally new insights from the governing gifts of the baptized.[35] No doubt it would be a daunting task given the present "sacred" structure of governance.

---

32. Ronald Rohlheiser, *The Holy Longing* (New York: Doubleday, 1999), 121.

33. See www.voiceofthefaithful.org.

34. www.voiceofthefaithful.org.

35 See William J. Rademacher, "A New Kind of Plenary Council?" *Church* 19 (Summer 2003), 28–31.

Peter Steinfels lists five major failures in the bishops' leadership during the sexual abuse scandal. He concludes that these failures were more systemic than personal.[36] And in any institution, religious or secular, reforming the system is always a major undertaking. Reform from inside the system is especially difficult. Institutional insiders do not willingly give up power and control. Thus, it's unrealistic to expect meaningful systemic reform to come from insiders like the U.S. Conference of Catholic bishops.

True reform will require faith, courage, and the new imagination and prayerful discernment of all the people of God. And, finally, it will require "the violent wind" and "the tongues of fire" of a New Pentecost. Chapters 3, 4, and 5 may point to a possible parish response to that Pentecostal Spirit.[37]

For Reflection and Discussion

1. What changes since Vatican II were the hardest to accept?

2. What changes surprised you the most?

3. How do you feel about your parish's approach to multiculturalism?

4. What can you do about the priest shortage?

5. Do you wonder if you have a vocation to be a "lay ecclesial minister"?

6. Do you feel called to be a volunteer minister in your parish?

7. How do you feel about the new role of women in the ministries of your own parish?

---

36. Steinfels, 309.

37. For more details on this turbulent postconciliar period, see David Gibson, *The Coming Catholic Church* (New York: HarperCollins, 2004), especially pp. 1–146.

CHAPTER 3

Parish Identity

We are "a people adrift." So it may be helpful to reflect on who we are. What are we called to do? What is the Catholic parish's identity? What is its mission? "If the church is to be the church," writes Avery Dulles, "it must have a clear sense of its own identity and mission."[1] The same is true of the Catholic parish.

Even if we do not feel adrift, we are certainly in transition.[2] So it may be helpful to figure out, transitioning from what to what? Identity, either our own or that of the parish, is not a static, unchangeable reality. In fact, we know from psychologists such as Sam Levinson and Erik Erikson that our own identity is fluid and constantly in a state of development. Life, and therefore our identity, has different stages or periods. Most importantly, it has difficult transitions from one stage to the next. Negotiating the specific transitions may bring on a painful crisis.

Of course, the parish is not just another human, though Christian, community. Vatican II in its *Dogmatic Constitution on the Church* is straightforward. The title of the very first chapter, "The Mystery of the Church," says it all: "The term 'mystery,'" reads the footnote, "indicates that the church, as a divine reality inserted into history, *cannot be fully captured by human thought or language.*"[3] This note reminds us all to be humble before this

---

1. As quoted in *The Resilient Church* (Garden City, NY: Doubleday, 1977), 26.

2. See Gerald Miller and Wilburn Stancil, eds., *Catholicism at the Millennium* (Kansas City, MO: Rockhurst University Press, 2001), especially Chapter 5.

3. See Chapter 2, note 4, regarding the Abbott Edition. Italics mine.

divine/human mystery called the church. The Catholic parish and its identity are part of that mystery.

We could well be tempted to give up before we start. Why try to describe the parish's identity when we know it's a mystery? Because we Christians believe that our mysteries are previews of the Infinite. Mysteries are divine doors partly open so that through our faith we can, even in this life, get a peek into that which "no eye has seen, nor ear heard" (1 Cor 2:9). While we cannot *fully* capture these mysteries in human words, we can, nevertheless, gain a glimpse of that eternal truth that Christ reveals to us even in this life. Jesus, the incarnation of God, brought a little of eternity to us. By meditating on our Lord's mysteries, we can, in the words of Saint Ambrose, "breathe in the fragrance of eternal life."

Our approach to the identity of the Catholic parish will have to be limited primarily to the visible, human part of the mystery of the parish. At the same time, we realize that in actual reality the parish's human and divine elements cannot be separated. Since the Incarnation, the human is the apt vehicle for the divine. Thus, these two elements never exist separately.

Many theologians have tried to gain insight into the mystery of the parish through the use of models.[4] Some of these models lean heavily on the 1917 Code of Canon Law and present the parish in its dependency on the diocesan church. Thus the identity of the parish is derivative of the diocesan church. Others, like Karl Rahner, emphasize "church from below" as opposed to "church from above." Still others, like Michael Winter, feel the modern U.S. parish is still shaped primarily by Catholic Europe when everybody was Catholic. He sees the parish primarily as a eucharistic community. Convinced that the size of the parish must be reduced, he feels the basic parish should be limited to twenty or thirty people. The *normal* celebration of the Eucharist should be in private houses.[5]

---

4. See especially Sabbas Kilian, OFM, *Theological Models for the Parish* (New York: Alba House, 1977); Charles Davis et al, *The Parish in the Modern World* (London: Sheed and Ward, 1965); Michael Winter, *Blueprint for a Working Church: A Study in New Pastoral Structures* (St. Meinrad, IN: Abbey Press, 1973); Karl Rahner, *The Shape of the Church to Come* (New York: Seabury Press, 1972); Alex Blochinger, *The Modern Parish Community*, Geofrey Steven, trans. (New York: P.J. Kenedy and Sons, 1965); Patrick Brennan, *Re-Imagining the Parish* (New York: Crossroad, 1991).

5. For more detailed description of these models, see William J. Rademacher, *Answers for Parish Councillors* (Mystic, CT: Twenty-Third Publications, 1981), 29–50.

All these discussions make helpful contributions. But there may be other ways to get to the identity of the parish.

New Marks for the Catholic Parish

Many Catholics understand the identity of the church through the four marks: one, holy, catholic, and apostolic. These four qualities of the church have been part of the Nicene Creed since 381, although they are not called marks. But these four qualities acquired a *quasi* sacred status as four marks when, in 1885, they became part of the *Baltimore Catechism*. After that, all U.S. Catholics who learned their catechism had to memorize these four marks. The catechism explained that it was through these four marks that our Catholic "church could easily be found and recognized by men." These four marks are also listed and explained in the revised *Catechism of the Catholic Church* (1994).

However, the church has not always limited the marks to a "sacred" four. Fifteenth- to seventeenth-century theologians described the identity of the church through a variety of marks, notes, or characteristics. Suarez, a Jesuit theologian, taught that there were eight; Cardinal Bellarmine described fifteen; another theologian thought there were a hundred. More recently these marks have also been called "the dimensions of the church."

So let's assume that a list of a variety of marks is still a good way to understand the identity of the parish. While the traditional four still apply to the modern Catholic parish, perhaps, after Vatican II, we can move beyond them. Maybe we can come to a better understanding of the parish's identity by reflecting on a variety of other marks. All these marks incorporate both divine and human elements, sometimes more of one than of the other. We cannot isolate one mark from the total mystery of the church. At the same time, we are aware that our poor human words cannot really capture the *fullness* of the mystery that is the Catholic parish. But even a peek into this mystery is an exciting revelation.

Word of God

Our faith tells us that our church, including our parish, is blessed with divine gifts, which will be only the barest beginning of the marks revealing the parish's identity. First on our list of gifts is the *word of God*. This word is not simply the printed word as contained in the Scripture, but also, and especially, the word made flesh, "full of grace and truth" dwelling among us (Jn 1:14). After the Resurrection, this word is alive as a power within the Christian community called the parish. Through this word Christ continues to be present within the baptized community as surely as he is present in the Eucharist. This is the first mark of the parish.

The word proclaimed during the Sunday liturgy elicits our faith response because it is the very word of God, now present in our midst. That word continues to call all the baptized gathered around the altar during the Sunday liturgy. It has a unique force and authority that transcends the human frailty of the proclaimer. It is one of the marks of every Catholic parish and therefore points to its identity.

More Organism than Organization

The parish community is also the *body of Christ.* "Now you are the body of Christ and individually members of it" (1 Cor 12:27). This is a second gift to the parish. It's an awesome thought, but the body of Christ constitutes part of our parish identity. The metaphor of the body had been used before Saint Paul by Seneca, a famous Roman philosopher, to apply to the body politic. Here Paul applies that same metaphor to the Christian community at Corinth. The meaning is clear: "All Christians are united as one body with Christ, because all of them share in the one life-giving power of the Spirit that comes from the Father through Christ and makes all who believe one with Christ and with one another."[6] When we say "Amen" while receiving Holy Communion, we are really saying, "Yes, I am a member of the body of Christ."

All the members of the body of the parish need each other as the hand needs the foot. "The eye cannot say to the hand, 'I have no need of you'" (1 Cor 12:21). The whole parish is a community of collaborative ministries, just as the members of the human body "minister" to each other. Thus, when one member of the parish body hurts, the whole body hurts. The parish is more organism than organization. It grows, gets old, is

6. Peter F. Ellis, *Seven Pauline Letters* (Collegeville, MN: Liturgical Press, 1982), 94.

reborn. Like any human body, it is vulnerable to all the pathologies of its culture. As an organism, it rightly celebrates the mysteries of life and death. *Organism* is part of its identity and, therefore, a second mark of the parish.

Variety of the Gifts of the Spirit

The parish is also blessed with the gifts of the Spirit. Paul's list of gifts is long and diverse but all the gifts are "activated by one and the same Spirit" (1 Cor 12:11). The gifts are given to all the baptized. They are more functions than offices. They do not depend on an ordination or commissioning ceremony. But just as in the human body, all these gifts need to be ordered to the upbuilding of the parish community. These *gifts of the Spirit* serve as a third mark of the parish.

Christian Community

The parish is a Christian community in process. In the Greek New Testament the word used for community is *koinonia*. Literally it means "a partnership, a sharing in, a fellowship in the spirit." In secular Greek, *koinonia* describes the marriage relationship. It conveys the intimacy of bed and board, of life together with all its joys and sorrows. The parish is a community in process because real community is always a difficult goal still to be achieved. The Christian community has to be built around the person of Jesus Christ, nothing less. The community's celebration of the full Eucharist is a crucial part of that Christ-centered building process.

Our U.S. culture presents almost insurmountable obstacles to the building of community. Individualism and the privatization of religion militate against the building of community as two mighty forces. Besides that, in an affluent society such as the U.S., people just don't need each other. They can afford to be independent. Everybody has their own television, car, computer, and cell phone. Poverty, on the other hand, creates an interdependence that can lead to the formation of community. Finally, sin militates against Christian community. Sin seeks the self rather than the good of the neighbor. Therefore it divides rather than unites. To build community, individual Christians need to live in a forgiving and reconciling relationship with God and with each other. They need a lot of compassion for the human part of their parish and for each other's human frailty. They need to be disposed to lay down their lives for others. Christian communities do not exist for themselves; they are always in service to the kingdom of God.

The size of the modern mega-parishes also is an obstacle to building a Christian community. Authors describing community speak of "face-to-face association…the small number of persons involved; the relative intimacy among the participants." Besides that, true community requires "a sense of reciprocity and belonging…a commitment to common goals, opportunities for personal exchange."[7] It should be clear from these descriptions that for most U.S. parishes this mark of their parish is still a goal to be achieved. Presently, most U.S. parishes can hardly be called bread-breaking communities like the house-churches of the early church. Nevertheless, *Christian community* is a fourth mark of the parish.

Faith

The fifth mark of the parish is *faith*, as a verb. The New Testament Greek *pisteuo* (I believe) means "I place my trust in," "I commit my life to," "I cast myself upon" God. Faith is not an object we possess, but part of who we are. Active believing is our distinguishing identity. It sets us apart and marks us as faith-filled disciples of Christ. As parishioners, we do not "commit our lives" to the church's human representatives, such as pastors or bishops. Our believing transcends the passing historical forms of institutional religion, including our parish. Since we carry our faith in fragile human vessels, our active believing is, of course, somewhat dependent on its human representatives. Thus the clerical sexual abuse crisis rocked the faith of many Catholics. But in the end, this crisis may purify our faith from its overdependence on the human. "Believing" means we "cast ourselves" on Christ, not on his human leaders, however anointed, however charismatic.

Baptismal Vocation

The Catholic parish is a community of the called. The parish is a portion of the new people of God, "a chosen race, a royal priesthood, a holy

---

7. Evelyn Whitehead, ed., *The Parish in Community and Ministry* (New York: Paulist Press, 1978), 42.

nation, God's own people" (1 Pet 2:9–10). "Christ instituted a new covenant…by calling together a people made up of Jew and Gentile, making them one, not according to the flesh but in the spirit."[8] Thus all the baptized in the parish have a vocation. Or better, they are being called daily as the lover calls the beloved.

First, the baptized are being called to discipleship. It is clear from Acts 6:1—21:16 that all the baptized are considered disciples of Jesus Christ. Christian discipleship shapes the parish community. Vocation, therefore, means a call to discipleship, a call that comes daily to all the baptized in the parish. Thus, we do not need to pray that God might call, for God does not cease to call. We need to pray that those called, all the baptized, answer God's call.

Discipleship will take various forms, and these forms may change often until death. A vocation is not the same as a career, a lifetime job, or a state of life, religious or secular. It's the Christian's *daily* response: "Here am I; send me!" (Isa 6:8). The Lord does not always send us to a church-defined vocation. Abram didn't have a clue about where God was sending him (Gen 12:1).

Second, the Catholic parish is called to holiness. Paul, writing to the Romans, begins with a simple greeting: "To all God's beloved in Rome, who are called to be saints" (Rom 1:7). Thus the call to holiness is not limited to the ordained or to the religious. "All the faithful of Christ of whatever rank or status are called to the fullness of the Christian life and to the perfection of charity."[9] That's the call to holiness. But holiness is not a destination; it's a way of life. It's the joyous daily acceptance of the gift of God's unconditional love in and through Christ. Prayer and spiritual exercises are forms of communion between lovers. They nourish the union with the Beloved. At the same time, they are the blessed fruit of that union. So we do not find holiness in a particular place such as a desert, a monastery, or a Catholic Mecca. Nor does it depend on vows. Nor do we earn it by doing a lot of "good deeds." We are not Pelagians. The grace of holiness is God's totally gratuitous gift.

---

8. Vatican II, *Dogmatic Constitution on the Church*, no. 9.

9. *Dogmatic Constitution*, no. 40.

Holiness, as pure grace, is a way of being. It's an earthly anticipation of that union with God that will last for eternity. Thus holiness and happiness go together. In fact, the saints' examples teach us that happiness is the fruit of holiness. "All the way to heaven is heaven," says Catherine of Siena. "A saint who is sad," writes Francis de Sales, "is a sad sort of saint." Knowing in our hearts that we are going the right way, with God pulling us along, is sheer joy. All the members of the parish know that they "are the temple of the living God…[and that God] will live in them and walk among them" (2 Cor 6:16). And so we come to the sixth mark of the Catholic parish: all members have a *religious vocation*, both to discipleship and to holiness.

Ecumenical Sisters and Brothers

The Catholic parish is ecumenical. After *Decree on Ecumenism* of Vatican II, it is just not possible for a parish to call itself Catholic without a commitment to ecumenism. We are certain now that "other churches or ecclesial communities are joined with us in the Holy Spirit, for to them he gives his gifts and graces and is thereby operative among them with his sanctifying power."[10] The decree tells us that "Catholics must assuredly be concerned for their separated brethren, praying for them, keeping them informed about the church, making the *first approaches toward them.*"[11] But the decree also advises that "Catholics must first make a careful appraisal of whatever needs to be renewed within the Catholic household itself."

The Catholic parish takes the first steps toward the members of other faiths not with a view to converting them, but to begin a dialogic relationship with them. Such relationships will surely lead to different forms of fruitful cooperation in the common Christian apostolate. Catholics and Protestants can easily work together on humanitarian issues such as poverty, ecology, civil rights, racial discrimination, peace movements, Habitat for Humanity, repeal of the death penalty, and Church Women United. All participants will discover again that the areas of mutual agreement on essentials outnumber those of disagreement. Such ecumenical dialogues no doubt will eventually lead to that day "when all Christians will be gath-

---

10. *Dogmatic Constitution*, no. 15.

11. *Decree on Ecumenism*, no. 4.

ered, in a common celebration of the Eucharist."[12] In the meantime, Catholic parishes can take the first steps without preconceived notions of the forms Christian unity may take. We may plant but God will give the growth (1 Cor 3:6) in God's own time and place. *Ecumenism* is a seventh mark of the parish.

Pilgrims

The Catholic parish is a pilgrim. As the Lord's disciples, we are exiles on this earth, on our way home. We are marked by a holy restlessness, still seeking the "city that is to come" (Heb 13:14). We are finite hearts yearning for the Infinite. "What pilgrim does not hasten homeward?" writes Cyprian. "Paradise is our true home. Many friends await us there—parents, brothers and sisters, sons and daughters." Like Paul, we are anxious to be "caught up to the third heaven" (2 Cor 12:2), there to be embraced totally and unconditionally by Infinite Love. This will be a love that purges all our earthbound sins, defects, and anxieties.

We are certainly familiar with the Catholic custom of thousands of pilgrims making a pilgrimage to Lourdes, Rome, Jerusalem, or Compostela. Many Catholics have an instinct of faith that being a pilgrim is part of their identity.

But being a pilgrim has profound spiritual meaning. Pilgrims travel light. They don't want to be encumbered with many possessions during their earthly journey. They are also sinners still on the way. They are still seeking holiness or at least some favor from the Lord. Before Vatican II the church often claimed to be a perfect society. Prone to triumphalism, it stressed its divine nature and forgot its sinful, human frailty. But Vatican II's *Dogmatic Constitution on the Church* devoted all of Chapter 7 to the "Pilgrim Church."

This pilgrim dimension corrects the former triumphalist tendency. It means a return to the still sinful members of the church. The people on pilgrimage need to show compassion for each other's frailty and imperfections. They have to help each other during the heat of the day and the cold of the night. The pilgrimage itself is the great equalizer. All suffer the same discouragement and, at times, disorientation when they have to search

---

12. *Decree on Ecumenism*, no. 4.

again for the right way. They need to return often to their only light on the journey, the light of Christ.

Thus, the parish, in Karl Rahner's delightful phrase, is "an unfinished symphony." It's always incomplete. Like the church itself, the parish is always dysfunctional.[13] Both weeds and wheat will grow until the harvest (Mt 13:30). So even our favorite parish always falls a little short. This earthly journey is burdened with all the sins and imperfections of the human condition. Shopping for the perfect parish is as useless as looking for the perfect wife or husband. It doesn't exist. A particular kind of Catholic may indeed feel he has a good reason to shop for the kind of Mass he likes: "A still, small voice of calm is what one Catholic yearned for, but his search brought him whooped Sanctuses and showbiz. Then he found a Mass at a convent."[14]

We go to Mass not to be catered to, but to be changed, to make contact with the living God through Jesus Christ. If we wanted to watch a showbiz comedian or indulge in a personality cult, we could stay home and watch television. Our shopping for a Mass or a parish may simply mean that we are infected with our culture's consumer pathology. We actually go to Mass to own our place in our frail pilgrim community, such as it is, including, unfortunately, the priest comedian or the "whooped" *sanctus*. We go to serve our poor community, not to be served. We go primarily to give and, only secondarily, to receive.

In the final analysis, we all belong where the sinners gather, where they begin their service by publicly confessing: "my fault…my most grievous fault,"[15] and then continue with: "Lord, I am not worthy." *One* of the reasons for going to church is well expressed by Rolheiser: "To go to church is to seek the therapy of a public life and to be part of that therapy for others. Simply put, I go to church so that other people might help me carry what is unhealthy inside me and so that I might help them carry what is unhealthy inside them."[16] That's what Christian pilgrims do.

---

13. See Michael Crosby, *The Dysfunctional Church* (Notre Dame, IN: Ave Maria Press, 1991).

14. Michael McMahon, "Rid Us of the Game Show Hosts," *The Tablet* 258 (April 17, 2004), 9.

15. Translated from the Spanish version: *"por mi culpa…por mi gran culpa."*

16. Ronald Rolheiser, *The Holy Longing*, 138.

To belong, heart and soul, to any parish requires compassion and forgiveness as a permanent disposition. The parish is only "the seed and beginning" of the kingdom of God. It's not the kingdom. Even when the kingdom arrives, it won't be a kingdom of angels. It will still have its human, "unfinished" component. Thus, *pilgrim* is the eighth mark of the parish.

Parish as Sacrament

In spite of its sinfulness, the Catholic parish is also a sacrament. We know from the *Dogmatic Constitution on the Church* of Vatican II that "the church is the universal sacrament of salvation"[17] We learned from our catechism that a sacrament is an outward sign that indicates the presence of the thing signified. "If a sign produces the thing made known," the catechism continues, "it is an effective sign (sacrament)." The parish, then, is a sign of Christ's presence in a specific time and place. Since it is an efficacious sign, it mediates Christ's saving grace in a particular part of the Lord's vineyard. All the baptized members of the parish are anointed as sacraments of saving grace. They share in the priesthood of Jesus Christ. Catholics meet saving grace primarily at the parish level. Through the Incarnation Christ has willed to be present through very human disciples who make up the body of Christ. This is an awesome mystery, but parishes need to get a grip on their true identity. The parish as *sacrament* is a ninth mark of the parish.

Agent of Change

The Catholic parish is an agent of change. When a Catholic parish moves into the neighborhood, "there'll be some changes." Catholic communities come into a neighborhood as signs of saving grace. They come with some serious mandates from the Lord: "You are the salt of the earth....You are the light of the world" (Mt 5:13, 14). "The kingdom of heaven is like yeast that woman took and mixed in with three measures of flour until all of it was leavened" (Mt 13:33). The yeast is a symbol for the power of God, working silently but effectively through all the baptized. The kingdom of God has not arrived yet. Until it does, Christians have a vocation to be the

---

17. *Dogmatic Constitution*, no. 48.

yeast of change within their culture and city. Paul provides the motivation for becoming a change agent: "The love of Christ urges us on" (2 Cor 5:14). All parishioners are the disciples of Christ who through them is renewing the face of the earth. It all begins in the parish.

A community of Christians, as agents of change, cannot cling to Christ's values without creating some impact on a culture that holds different, or even opposite, values. Christians do not follow the crowd; they follow Christ. These different values may be pro-life, pro-human rights, pro-human dignity, pro-equality, pro-labor unions, pro-social justice, pro-ecology, pro-Pax Christi in time of war. But a community clinging to these kinds of values will make a difference in the neighborhood. "He has sent me to bring good news to the oppressed, to bind up the broken-hearted, to proclaim liberty to the captives, and release to the prisoners" (Isa 61:1). When Catholics leave the house they don't leave their Christian values behind. So *change* agent is the tenth mark of the parish.

Christian Hospitality

The eleventh mark of the parish is *hospitality*. Already in 1 Timothy 3:2 we see that one of the qualities demanded of an overseer, or bishop, is hospitality. It's clear that hospitality was an important virtue in all the churches. Paul tells the Romans to "contribute to the needs of the saints; extend hospitality to strangers" (Rom 12:13). And 1 Peter 4:9 tells us to "be hospitable to one another without complaining." In the early church, before Constantine (d. 337), house-churches were the norm. Christians gathered for the "breaking of the bread" in private houses. So the hosts or hostesses were expected to offer the hospitality of their own homes for Christian worship.

The rule of Saint Benedict (d. 543) on the "Reception of Guests" reveals how important the virtue of hospitality was for the early church and for all the Benedictine communities. The rule on reception begins: "All guests are to be received as Christ himself....And to all fitting honor shall be shown; but most of all, to servants of the faith and to pilgrims....The abbot as well as the *whole congregation* shall wash the feet of all the guests."[18]

---

18. Henry Bettenson, ed., *Documents of the Christian Church*, (New York: Oxford University Press, 1967), 124 (italics mine).

This mark of hospitality for the Catholic parish today should not surprise us. After all, we re-enact the Lord's washing of the feet every Holy Thursday. We regularly hear the parable of the Good Samaritan proclaimed from our pulpits. Then we hear that blunt ending: "Go and do likewise" (Lk 10:23–37). We also regularly hear the parable of the return of the Prodigal Son. It ends with that grand celebration for the whole household: "This son of mine was dead and is live again; he was lost and is found" (Lk 15:11–32). These gospel examples had a powerful effect in forming the early church with a strong orientation toward Christian hospitality.

But to be truly Christian, the parish hospitality must include not just fellow Catholics or Protestants, but "outsiders." Christian hospitality is a unifying force. It embraces Jews and Muslims, agnostics, atheists, secularists, and the declared enemies of religion. After all, the Good Samaritan who is presented as our example in Jesus' parable is an outcast, an alien and heretic.[19]

Almsgiving

The twelfth mark of the parish is *almsgiving*. We may complain about how many times the collection basket is passed during the Sunday liturgy, but almsgiving was certainly a mark of the early church. In the gospels we proclaim on Sunday, Jesus often speaks about "alms" or "almsgiving" (Mt 6:2; Lk 11:41; 12:33). So we are not surprised to see in the Acts of the Apostles, the history of the early church, that almsgiving is also an important part of the practice of the early churches. Alms or "almsdeeds" are mentioned seven times in Acts. A certain disciple, Tabitha, "was devoted to good works and acts of charity" (Acts 9:36). During the reign of Claudius there was a great famine all over the world. "The disciples determined that according to their ability, each would send relief to the believers living in Judea" (Acts 11:28–29). Thus, almsgiving constitutes an essential part of the Christian ethical life for Luke. He challenges "those who have, to share with those who have not."[20] Cyprian, the bishop of Carthage, wrote a whole treatise, *Works and Almsgiving*, during a devastating plague in 253.

---

19. For more details on hospitality, see Thomas Richstatter, "The Ministry of Hospitality," *America* 190 (May 3, 2004), 12–14.

20. Raymond E. Brown, Joseph A. Fitzmeyer, and Roland E. Murphy, *The New Jerome Biblical Commentary* (Englewood Cliffs, NJ: Prentice Hall, 1988), 703.

Paul, too, gives rather specific instructions about the "collection for the saints" (1 Cor 16:1–4). In his letter to the Romans he once again makes an important point about the collection, saying the Christians at "Macedonia and Achaia have been pleased to share their resources with the poor among the saints at Jerusalem" (Rom 15:26). For Paul, the collection had theological significance.[21] If the Jews accepted a contribution from the hated Gentiles, they were accepting those Gentiles as equal members in the new Christian community, now composed of Jews and Gentiles. The giving and receiving of the collection was a distinguishing mark of an authentic fellowship within the Christian community.

Healing Community

The parish is called to be a healing community. From the ten lepers (Lk 17:12) to the man born blind (Jn 9:1–34), the four gospels present the historical Jesus as a healer. And Jesus' instructions to his disciples are clear enough: "Cure the sick...cleanse the lepers" (Mt 10:8). So we're not surprised to read in 1 Corinthians 12:9 that the Holy Spirit gives the "gifts of healing" to the baptized.

A parish community built around Jesus Christ will have to be a public sign, or sacrament, of a healing Jesus and the healing gifts of the Spirit. In the New Testament the Greek word used for healing is *therapeuo*, which also means "I care for, attend, serve, or treat." Our English words "therapy" and "therapeutic," without their modern professional connotation, are fairly accurate descriptions of the word used in the New Testament for Jesus' healing. Thus, we ought not to restrict Jesus' healing or the gifts of healing to the physical. Jesus' healing was more [w]holistic, including the spiritual and emotional. Thus, the parish community is called to heal the sick, the mentally ill, the hurting marriages and families, the sex, drug, and alcohol addicted. Even when the parish hires professional help, the whole parish still remains a healing, therapeutic community. The sacrament of the anointing of the sick is the visible, outstretched arm of the whole parish community. *Healing* is the thirteenth mark of the Catholic parish.

---

21. For more details on the theology of the collection in Paul, see Keith Nickle, *The Collection* (Naperville, IL: Alec R. Allenson, 1966), 100–43.

Multiethnic, Multiracial, Multicultural Parish

The modern Catholic parish is multicultural. Quite simply, this is today's blessed reality. While our new immigrants cling to their own religious and ethnic symbols and languages, they also cling to their own cultures. (Those who remain unconvinced need to spend just one month in Los Angeles.)

Multiculturalism is a welcome but difficult challenge for the "catholicity" of the modern Catholic parish. Building a true Christian community across different cultures may seem like an impossible dream at times. But with the shortage of indigenous priest presiders, it makes no theological sense to build a separate parish for each new culture. A truly Catholic, bread-breaking community welcomes all colors and cultures to share their bread at their common table. To do otherwise would betray the meaning of Christian community. So *multiculturalism*, with all its tensions and blessings, is the fourteenth mark of the parish.

Dialogic Parish

Finally, the parish is *dialogic*. It listens. It listens hard. Then, and only then, it speaks. The *Pastoral Constitution on the Church in the Modern World* of Vatican II wanted to express its "solidarity with the entire human family…by engaging it in conversation about…various problems."[22] Speaking of atheists, the same constitution urges the faithful to engage them in "a sincere and prudent dialogue…for the rightful betterment of this world."[23] True dialogue is a tough discipline to learn and then practice on a daily basis.[24] But once achieved, true dialogue melts prejudice. It paves the way for healthy Christian relationships. By its dialogue the parish proclaims publicly that fellow humans can live together in peace and harmony in a war-torn, pluralistic world. It proclaims, finally, that all humans are precious, redeemed as they are by the precious blood of the Son of God.

As a close-knit bread-breaking community, the parish is constantly in dialogue about its own internal affairs: How to restructure to accomplish the mission in a given time and place? What are the special qualities of leadership needed for the parish and for the diocese? It conducts open dis-

---

22. Preface, no. 3.

23. No. 21.

24. See Ruel L. Howe, *The Miracle of Dialogue* (New York: Seabury Press, 1963), 78–81.

cussions about selecting new pastors and new bishops. Through dialogue the parish prepares for the diocesan synod and selects its delegates to the synod itself. The Code of Canon Law allows "lay members of the Christian faithful" to participate in the diocesan synod (canon 463, 2). The open parish forum is an annual event facilitated by the parish pastoral council. It's a dialogue with the whole parish.

The parish also initiates dialogue with those outside of the parish, such as Jews,[25] Buddhists, Muslims, agnostics, and even the declared enemies of religion.[26] Dialogue enables peaceful coexistence. It heals wounds, real or imagined. It builds the conditions for peace rather than for war. *Dialogue* is the fifteenth mark of the Catholic parish.

There are many other marks of the Catholic parish. Thus, we would certainly expect the parish community to be marked as a forgiving and reconciling community. The prodigal son or daughter can always come home to a warm, forgiving welcome, followed by a celebration. But the fifteen marks described above may provide a better understanding of the identity of the Catholic parish. On the other hand, we continually define our identity by our everyday actions and by our zealous commitment to a dream yet to be fulfilled. So to complete the picture of our parish's identity, we also need to reflect on the mission, dreams, and goals of the parish.

For Reflection and Discussion

1. How does your parish measure up to the above fifteen marks?
2. Which of the fifteen marks needs the most attention in your parish?
3. Are there any other marks you would add to the list?
4. What are some of the obstacles you meet in the practice of ecumenism?
5. Would you like to serve on a parish committee to promote dialogue with Jews and Muslims? Why or why not?
6. What are the obstacles in your parish in building community? Are there any indications of factions? Of polarization? Other obstacles?

---

25. For dialogue with Jews, see Vatican II's *Declaration on the Relationship of the Church to Non-Christian Religions*, and Peter Stanford, "Ways to Say 'Shalom,'" *The Tablet* 258 (May 15, 2004), 14–15.

26. See Wayne Teasdale, *Catholicism in Dialogue* (Lanham, MD: Sheed and Ward, 2004), 115–29.

CHAPTER 4

The Mission of the Parish

The distinction between identity and mission may, at first, seem arbitrary. Mission often flows from identity. But the mission also helps form identity. We recognize part of the plumber's identity through his work as a plumber. But still, we don't limit his identity to his plumbing. We also recognize him as a human person, as a father, and so on. Often mission and identity are so closely linked to each other that they overlap. In practice we often recognize who we are by what we do. The same holds true for the Catholic parish.

If a man from Mars were to land on a typical parish parking lot on a typical day, he might well be impressed, both by the size of the parish plant and by all the activity. Lots of people coming and going: some to or from classes in the school, some to the drama practice just beginning in the parish hall, some to meetings, and others to a funeral just now starting in church. Our man from Mars might ask a passing parishioner: "What's all this activity for?" He might actually get this answer: "Somehow it's all for the kingdom of God." Or again, another might answer: "We're just trying to be church. We're trying to be true to our parish identity."

Both answers serve as a basic orientation to the mission of the parish. Just like the church, the parish is always in service to the kingdom of God. And for the parish, being true to its identity will always be part of its mission. That is simply a question of being a faithful servant of the Lord.

It may also be helpful to remember that the parish, like the church, has an inner and an outer mission.[1] During the Vatican II discussions, the bish-

---

1. See Foster and Sweetser, *Transforming the Parish*, 15–171.

50

ops distinguished the church *ad intra* and the church *ad extra*. The parish needs to be concerned about its own people, its own parish community, and, especially, about the kind of sign or image it presents to the public. It can be a warm, welcoming sacrament to the stranger or it can *appear* to be a hypocritical, self-serving, money-grabbing institution. So when we concentrate on the parish's outer mission, we cannot forget its inner ministry.

To Be a Eucharistic Community

Beyond the basic orientation to mission outlined above, there are other, more specific, goals within this parish mission. First, the parish has a mission to be what it celebrates. Now and forever, the parish is word and sacrament. Thus, it is always listening and responding to the word and then breaking and sharing the bread. Just as today's disciples share the bread, so they share their faith, their prayer, and their very lives in their workaday world.

The Eucharist is food for the journey, that is, the journey to spiritual wholeness. But, as a celebration, it is also an empowering community experience. It reactivates the dying, rising, and anointing of our baptism. Each eucharistic celebration recommissions today's disciples in Christ's priestly, prophetic, and kingly mission. For this reason all who leave church on Sunday can say with Saint Paul: "It is no longer I who live, but it is Christ who lives in me" (Gal 2:20). The Catholic parish cannot become a mere word community and still remain faithful to the Catholic tradition. The first disciples "devoted themselves to the apostles' teaching and fellowship, to the breaking of bread and the prayers" (Acts 2:42). So it must always be for all of the Lord's disciples.

To Proclaim the Good News

The second mission of the parish is to proclaim and teach the good news of salvation. The parish does this more by deed than by word. But here the parish has a double duty: first, to teach the believers in order to intensify their faith and, second, to proclaim the good news to those who have never heard it.

The parish teaches its own believers through its Catholic school and through its faith formation programs for children, teenagers, and adults. These programs include regular classes and special preparation for the celebration of the sacraments: baptism, reconciliation, first communion, confirmation, and marriage. The parish teaches every Sunday through the celebration of the liturgy, the homilies, and the special feast days of the liturgical calendar. From cradle to grave, Catholics need to grow in their faith. To neglect growth in the faith is to accept a state of underdevelopment in the faith. Trying to live an adult life in today's world with a childhood faith will always lead to shipwreck.

But the parish has a further responsibility to be a missionary to those who have never heard the good news. Vatican II teaches clearly: "It is plain, then, that missionary activity wells up from the church's innermost nature and spreads abroad her saving faith."[2] In other words, missionary activity flows from the parish's very identity. This is not a question of simply putting money into the special collections for the missions. All parishioners are missioners. This may mean that within a few blocks from their parish church they may clothe the naked, give drink to the thirsty, feed the hungry, or welcome the stranger (Mt 25:35–36). Or, it may mean a simple dialogue with an agnostic neighbor. In an age of proliferation of "talk shows," simple, but real, listening is sometimes the greatest gift a missioner can offer to a searching neighbor. The detachment and self-sacrifice required in this gift is saving grace in a world aching to be heard.

In recent years some parishes have launched very successful evangelization programs. Reverend Patrick Brennan describes the *oikos* (household) evangelization program of St. Boniface Parish in Miami.[3] It's based on household relationships broadly understood. It begins with kinship, the family members, then moves to location, the neighborhood, then to common interests, such as hobbies, and finally to "vocation," or the people with whom we work on a daily basis. Evangelization, whatever its organizational form, will always be part of every parish's outer mission.

To Worship through the Parish Liturgy

Third, the parish is called to worship the living God. This is the beating heart of its mission. Worship establishes a right relationship between crea-

---

2. *Decree on the Missionary Activity of the Church*, no. 6.

3. Patrick Brennan, *Re-Imagining the Parish* (New York: Crossroad, 1991), 63–66.

ture and Creator. For through Christ, the God-man, we finite creatures can actually relate to an infinite God. Through Christ, present among us, we can offer praise and thanksgiving that we poor, sinful humans are loved by an infinite Lover. This love is a gift beyond measure in human terms. It is the source of our Christian dignity and self-worth. Praising and thanking an infinitely generous and loving God will forever be the mission of the redeemed. Mere human words fail us when we try to describe the mystery of an all-holy, infinite God loving us while we are ungrateful sinners. Offering a liturgy of praise and thanksgiving will forever be the mission of all the baptized. That's why we are rightly called a eucharistic people.

This mission means that all the baptized actively participate in the parish's worship. There are no passive observers. We don't just go to Mass. We become one with Christ in offering ourselves, heart and soul, to be a living part of the mystery. Our prayers and songs of praise are acts of our total engagement with the paschal mystery. These are the doors through which we pass to a new life of grace. Our mission is to celebrate both who we are and what we do.

To Build a Christian Community

The fourth mission of the parish is to build a truly Christian community. This is the first item on the agenda for every parish meeting. It's part of the parish's inner mission. If the parish fails in this mission, it will fail in everything else. Failure in this is a public betrayal of the meaning of the breaking and sharing of the bread on Sunday. The members of the community must generate and nurture those inner dynamics that build and bond a Christian community: continuing forgiveness and reconciliation; laying down their lives for each other; praying and singing together; caring for the sick and elderly; welcoming the poor to the community table. In the midst of it all there must be leadership in the image of Christ. For no community will long survive as a Christian community without exemplary Christian leadership.

But a Christian community never remains an inward-turning community. In the model of Jesus, it's always laying down its life for others. It never exists for itself. By its very nature as a *Christian* community it gives birth to a variety of ministries. "Community must be understood as a spirit to be created, as an inspiration to bend one's constant efforts to overcome barriers between persons and to generate a relationship of solidarity and reciprocity."[4] Building these relationships of solidarity is best achieved through collaborative ministries, working together in the Lord's vineyard bearing "the burden of the day and the scorching heat" (Mt 20:12).

To Minister to the Church and to the World

The fifth mission of the parish is to offer Christian service. The wonderful Greek word used for service in the New Testament is *diakonia*. The verb *diakoneo* means "to wait at table." It referred particularly to the slave who poured out the wine to the dinner guests. While this Greek word had a variety of meanings, depending on the context, the image of the slave and his unpaid labor was never far removed. Perhaps the best insight into the meaning of *diakonia* comes from the example of Jesus himself during the Last Supper: "Then he poured water into a basin and began to wash the disciples' feet and to wipe them with the towel that was tied around him" (Jn 13:5). Foot-washing was the normal gesture of hospitality performed by slaves. But *diakonia* in its non-religious sense was also used for the service of the barber, the cook, the maid, the assistant helmsman, and the spearman who tortured the prisoners.[5]

The example of Jesus at the Last Supper adds a new meaning to service. Jesus was going to die on the morrow, giving his life to redeem all of humankind. So his foot washing is part of his last will and testament. Jesus himself gives us the meaning of his foot-washing example: "Do you know what I have done to you? You call me Teacher and Lord—and you are right, for that is what I am. So if I, your Lord and Teacher, have washed your feet, you also ought to wash one another's feet. For I have set you an example, that you also should do as I have done to you" (Jn 13:12–15).

The Lord's command still applies to the modern Catholic parish. Foot washing, of course, serves as a symbol of the kind of humble service Christians are called to offer to the world around them. This symbol highlights the Christians' inner motivation, their selfless, tender care in offering

---

4. Gregory Baum, *New Horizon* (New York: Paulist Press, 1972), 141.

5. William J. Rademacher, *Lay Ministry* (Eugene, OR: Wipf and Stock, 2002), 40.

service. But in our Christian context it is theologically more descriptive to name our Christian service ministry. For Paul, *diakonia* is ministry. He uses this Greek word in his letter to the Romans (12:7). Here he calls teaching a *ministry*. He uses this word in both letters to the Corinthians (1 Cor 16:15 and 2 Cor 4:1) and again in his letters to the Ephesians (4:12) and Colossians (4:17). Significantly, he uses *diakonia* in his famous list of charismatic gifts in 1 Corinthians 12. It's clear from Paul's letters that all the baptized in the parish are called to ministry. Thus we have eucharistic ministers, prison ministers, migrant ministers, health care ministers, and the like.

To Interpret the Signs of the Times

The sixth mission of the parish is "the duty of scrutinizing the signs of the times and of interpreting them in the light of the gospel."[6] This mission clearly affects the parish's relationship with the culture and world around it. For many years Catholic parishes in the U.S. were in a defensive mode with regard to the world. It was "us" against "them" (Protestants). In fact, U.S. Catholics suffered much from nativist hostility in the 1850s and beyond. Understandably, they felt like a persecuted minority. But this defensive mode also brought with it a negative attitude toward the world itself. The simplistic, dualist temptation of the fundamentalists is never far away: "We are the good guys; all those others are the evil ones."

With its *Pastoral Constitution on the Church in the Modern World*, Vatican II called for a less condemnatory, more positive view of the modern world. (It's important to note that Vatican II calls this document a constitution, not merely a decree or declaration.) This constitution, like the books of Genesis and Wisdom, sees a lot of good in the divinely created world: "God saw everything that he had made, and indeed, it was very good" (Gen 1:31). "For you love all things that exist, and detest none of the things that you have made" (Wis 11:24). This same constitution also reflects Pope John XXIII's positive teaching in his two major encyclicals, which often mention "the signs of the times." It recognizes the many positive "advances in the historical, social, and psychological sciences."[7] Besides that, it affirms in a

---

6. *Pastoral Constitution on the Church in the Modern World*, no. 4.

7. Donald Campion, *Introduction to the Pastoral Constitution*, Abbott edition, 185.

very positive tone, "the human race has passed from a rather static concept of reality to a more dynamic, evolutionary one."[8]

What does this mean for parishes scrutinizing the signs of the times? It brings a difficult challenge for prayerful discernment. The times, as always, will bring both the good and the bad—often mixed up. The church has no monopoly on saving grace. The power and presence of the Holy Spirit cannot be confined to institutional boundaries, secular or ecclesiastical. "The wind blows where it chooses" (Jn 3:8). Thus, the times can bring the good, even in the secular world, where and when we least expect it. So the constitution advises: "We must therefore recognize and understand the world in which we live, its expectations, its longings, and its often dramatic characteristics."[9]

On the other hand, the evil demonic power is also alive and well in the same world. "Although man was created in a state of holiness, at the very dawn of history man abused his liberty, at the urging of personified evil."[10] And this personified evil still roams this world until the coming of the kingdom in fullness. We think of 9/11 and the thousands killed in New York's Twin Towers. We think of the pathologies of our own U.S. culture, such as racism, corruption, consumerism, commercialism, and the growing gulf between the rich and poor.

While scrutinizing the signs of the times will always remain a difficult mission for the parish, the *Pastoral Constitution* itself provides a lot of help. It provides a fairly long list of the good in the modern world: "The human race is passing through a new stage in its history....Never has the human race enjoyed such an abundance of wealth, resources, and economic power....Technology is now transforming the face of the earth....New and more efficient media of social communication....A more critical ability to distinguish religion from a magical view of the world and from superstitions....Advances in biology, psychology, and the social sciences."[11] "The body is good and honorable since God has created it and will raise it up

---

8. *Pastoral Constitution*, no. 5.

9. *Pastoral Constitution*, no. 4.

10. *Pastoral Constitution*, no.13.

11. *Pastoral Constitution*, nos. 5, 6, and 7.

on the last day."[12] "Conscience is the most secret core and sanctuary of man."[13] "Authentic freedom is an exceptional sign of the divine image within man."[14]

But the same constitution is also realistically aware of many negative, evil elements in the modern world: "Fundamental personal rights are not yet being universally honored. Such is the case of a woman who is denied the right and freedom to choose a husband, to embrace a state of life, or to acquire an education or cultural benefits equal to those recognized for men."[15]

"Significant differences crop up too between races and between various kinds of social orders, between wealthy nations and those which are less influential or are needy."[16] "Man's freedom has been damaged by sin."[17] "Atheism must be accounted among the most serious problems of this age."[18] "Insults to human dignity, infamies, such as subhuman living conditions, arbitrary imprisonment, deportation, slavery, prostitution, the selling of women and children; as well as disgraceful working conditions, where men are treated as mere tools for profit, rather than as free and responsible persons."[19] "Abortion and infanticide are unspeakable crimes."[20] "The magnified power of humanity threatens to destroy the race itself."[21] With "ongoing wars or threats of them, the whole human family has reached an hour of supreme crisis."[22]

It's clear from the notes to this constitution that the council had no intention of providing a complete list of all the evils afflicting the world. In fact, one note clearly states that the "people of God must labor to dis-

---

12. *Pastoral Constitution*, no. 14.
13. *Pastoral Constitution*, no. 16.
14. *Pastoral Constitution*, no. 17.
15. *Pastoral Constitution*, no. 29.
16. *Pastoral Constitution*, no. 8.
17. *Pastoral Constitution*, no. 17.
18. *Pastoral Constitution*, no. 19.
19. *Pastoral Constitution*, no. 27.
20. *Pastoral Constitution*, no. 51.
21. *Pastoral Constitution*, no. 37.
22. *Pastoral Constitution*, no. 77.

cern the working of God's will from that of the Evil One." For this reason this fifth mission of the Catholic parish will, no doubt, be the most difficult. But as always, the parish has the help of the Holy Spirit and the teaching of the magisterium. Whatever the crisis, the Holy Spirit does not abandon the church or the parish.

"As Men Who Will Have to Give Account"

The seventh mission of the parish is to hold all its ministers accountable to the people of God, as we read in Hebrews 13:17. This is part of its inner mission. All Christian ministry is public. And there is no Lone Ranger ministry in the Catholic Church. All ministers, including lay ecclesial ministers, deacons, religious, priests, bishops, and popes are accountable, first of all, to Jesus Christ in whose name all Christian ministry is offered. Second, they are accountable to their own specific ecclesial communities. They are missioned, or sent out, by their community and report back to it by being accountable to it. This is the community, the body of Christ, that supports their ministry and discerns its usefulness for the upbuilding of the local church.[23] True Christian ministry will always remain servant leadership. And servants are always accountable for their service.[24]

The recent clergy sexual abuse scandal makes this particular mission of the parish all the more urgent. Accountability of all ministers, ordained or not, could be achieved through annual reviews and evaluations administered by diocesan and parish pastoral councils.[25] (University professors are routinely evaluated twice a year, at the end of each semester.) These evaluations could be sent to a diocesan personnel commission, assuming this body truly represents all the people of God: laity, priests, and religious. The members would need to have special competence in personnel matters. These consultative structures might need delegated executive authority on an ad hoc basis to deal adequately with the serious problems these evalua-

---

23. For more details on the principles of Christian ministry, see Rademacher, *Lay Ministry*, 46–47.

24. See Francis Oakley and Bruce Russett, eds., *Governance, Accountability, and the Future of the Catholic Church* (New York: Continuum International Publishing Group, 2004), especially Chapter 13, "A Haze of Fiction."

25. Regular self-evaluations by the parish ministers shared in a group would create a healthy attitude toward the evaluation process itself. Forster and Sweetser (*Transforming the Parish*) provide a simple but very helpful form for "The Self-Evaluation of Parish Ministries," 234–35.

tions present (canon 137). Because of the public nature of all ministry and the sacred rights of the people of God to competent and effective ministry, secrecy, denial, and cover-up could never become part of the system. Pastoral councils and personnel commissions are also publicly accountable to the people of God. The old and highly honored principle of fraternal/sisterly correction flows from the very nature of the Christian community: "Be on your guard! If another member of the church sins against you, go and point out the fault when the two of you are alone" (Lk 17:3; Mt 18:15).

All deacons, priests, bishops, religious, and laity will need to learn a lesson from Paul. He "opposed [Cephas] to his face" when his Jewish party was "not acting consistently with the truth of the gospel" (Gal 2:11–14). In politics or religion, loyalty to the truth always trumps loyalty to persons whatever their rank or charism. No doubt clericalism, the "original sin," will have to undergo a radical conversion.[26]

The process of fraternal/sisterly correction will always be a delicate one. First, the correctors need to be humbly aware of their own frail, fallible, and sinful condition. Second, they need to be reasonably certain that their effort at correction will be received as a gift, a Christian act of love of neighbor. Even so, the process will be difficult in our individualistic culture.

The British Parliament holds its prime minister accountable every Wednesday in a public question and answer period. These sessions are broadcast on public television. It's a weekly demonstration that public servants are accountable to their people for their ministry. No doubt Catholic parishes living in a democracy can devise some way for holding their own servant pastors and bishops publicly accountable to the people of God. So far, diocesan and parish pastoral councils, which by law are "consultative only," have not made much progress in achieving this public accountability. But achieving truly accountable servant leadership remains an important mission of every parish.

The people of the parish and its parish pastoral council will need to do considerable prayerful discernment to determine their specific faith response to the seven missions outlined above. The printed word can never capture the full mystery of the parish, either in its identity or in its

---

26. See David Gibson, *The Coming Catholic Church* (San Francisco: HarperCollins, 2004), especially 197–219.

mission. But these poor words are offered in the prayerful hope that they will be some help to the people of God in finding the right road on their pilgrim journey, a road that leads to that kingdom "already present in mystery. When the Lord returns it will be brought into full flower."[27]

For Reflection and Discussion

1. How does your parish carry out the seven missions outlined above?
2. What forms of accountability for ministers do you have in place in your parish?
3. What other missions would you add?
4. Which mission gets priority in the parish budget? Why?
5. Does your parish pastoral council have a mission statement? Does it need a review? Why or why not?
6. Discuss your parish's inner and outer missions. Which gets the most emphasis? Why?

27. *Pastoral Constitution*, no. 39.

CHAPTER 5

A Vision for Parish Planning

"Your old men shall dream dreams, and your young men shall see visions" (Joel 2:28).

We are a people on pilgrimage. So where is our pilgrimage going? And how do we get there? What's our plan? Visioning and planning for the Catholic parish during a time of crisis is a bold and risky undertaking. Both within the U.S. culture and within the Catholic Church some mighty forces for change are at work. One would need Solomon's wisdom to predict how these forces will interact and play out in the turbulent years ahead.

Chapters 3 and 4 discussed parish identity and mission. Now it's time to discuss the parish plan. For many parishes the plan is the fruit of a goal-setting workshop. Some goals may have a time limit of three to five years, but all goals flow from a common vision. Our parish pilgrimage has a destination and a plan to get there. The main purpose of the plan is to focus all parish gifts and energies in the same direction. Without such a plan the parish becomes weak clay that will be shaped by whatever forces each new crisis unleashes.

As Christians we believe firmly that the power of the Holy Spirit is a continuing force always guiding our church and our parish into a new era of life and vigor. The Holy Spirit still gives "the utterance of knowledge" (1 Cor 12:8) to the baptized. May we not prayerfully hope that the Spirit's wisdom will inspire all of us to shape our common vision and our plan for the future of our parish?

We can well agree with a recent Catholic editorial:

> The parish of the future is full of promise, but the period of transition will necessarily be painful, as Catholics shed a number of assumptions with which they grew up. Like the embryonic church gathered in the Upper Room in Jerusalem, they are waiting for new life.[1]

Our vision and plan need to be the fruit of our common prayerful discernment both on the truths of revelation and our graced human experience. We also need to be faithful to all the principles of discipleship. We need to build our vision and plan for the future of our parish with the living stones left to us by the Lord and his teaching church through the centuries. Perhaps we can all be like "the master of a household who brings out of his treasure what is new and what is old" (Mt 13:52).

We can vision out of the box only to a certain point. In our planning process we need to remember certain theological presuppositions:

1. Our vision will be evolving since each new generation of Christians needs to do its own prayerful discernment in view of new inspirations of the Holy Spirit, new historical conditions, and the changing worldview. Thus our parish plan, while firm, is not written on stone tablets.

2. In the church there is an important distinction between dogma and discipline. Celibacy is a discipline and, therefore, can be changed; the Trinity is dogma and cannot be changed. Even unchanging dogma, however, can be understood and interpreted in a new way. Unchanging dogma may also require a new language to preserve the original truth in a new generation. Thus the church changed "Holy Ghost" to "Holy Spirit."

3. Regarding law, custom, and discipline, what was developed under the inspiration of the Holy Spirit in one period of history can, responding to the same Spirit, be un-developed in another period when the original historical conditions have changed.

4. Our parish, as a living organism, must obey the law of all organisms: It must change and adapt or die.

---

1. "Let Us Have a Vision, Please," *The Tablet* 258 (March 27, 2004), 3.

5. In our legalistic culture it's helpful to remember that a conciliar constitution has the force of all constitutions. That is, it shapes and interprets the law, not vice versa. Within these guidelines our parish planning can be fairly open-ended.

Small Christian Communities

The future parish may need to restructure itself. This is an ongoing process in the life of the parish and a wonderful sign of that life. In view of the growing shortage of priest presiders, the need to restructure the parish is perhaps more urgent today than ever before. The many reasons for this restructuring of the parish go well beyond the scope of this chapter.[2]

Today's custom of creating more and more mega-parishes by merging and consolidating may be a temporary solution, but it is not the final answer. It creates more anonymity and diminishes the community building powers of the eucharistic celebration: singing together, mutual forgiveness, the sign of peace, and the sharing of the cup and bread among disciples, the sisters and brothers in the Lord. Recent research (2003) indicates "that restructured (merged) parishes receive significantly lower contributions per household than those with resident priest pastors."[3] There is an important message here.

Future parishes will plan to adopt modified versions of the base Christian communities (CEBs) of Latin America.[4] These base communities received the blessing and support of the Latin American Bishops Conference held in Medellin, Colombia, in 1968, and again at a similar conference held in Puebla, Mexico, in 1979. Meanwhile, in North America we see a continuing growth of these small Christian communities both in the U.S. and Canada. Over half of the parishes in the U.S. have already started some form of these small Christian communities. They do theological reflection on the relationship of their faith to life, on their call to discipleship and ministry. They are parish based with about eight to twelve

---

2. See "Diocesan Experiences in Parish Restructuring," *The CARA Report*, 9 (Spring 2004), 1, see especially "Advice for Restructuring from Dioceses that Have Done So," 11.

3. *The CARA Report*, 9 (Summer 2003), 5.

4. See Arthur Baranowski, *Creating Small Faith Communities* (Cincinnati, OH: St. Anthony Messenger Press, 1993), especially 1–63.

members in each group. Many of these groups are guided and encouraged by the National Pastoral Life Center in New York City.

Carolyn Butler, a member of a base community program organized by the Diocese of Westminster, England, describes her experience:

> These small groups are the powerhouse of the future parish. They are replacing some of the more traditional groups and providing the parish with much-needed foot soldiers. It is primarily through meeting each other, talking, and praying together that people feel sufficiently supported and emboldened to do more than simply go to Mass.[5]

With the formation of these kinds of small communities, Catholic parishes will have a multitude of small cells breathing new life into the larger parish community. To use the words of the 1987 Synod of Bishops, the parish will become "a dynamic community of communities."

Our Parish and the Proper Development of the Culture

Our vision and parish plan, while guided by the truths of revelation and the Catholic tradition, need to respond to and interact with today's U.S. culture. The *Pastoral Constitution on the Church in the Modern World* devotes a whole chapter to "The Proper Development of Culture." Our church, unlike the Amish and Mennonites, does not support the formation of a ghetto Catholic culture. We are called by the Lord to be the salt and the yeast within our existing culture, such as it is.

But that is a formidable challenge. Our culture is an evolving conglomeration of positive and negative elements. So we need to discern what elements deserve our blessing and support and what elements deserve an exorcism and a prophetic response. When we exorcise our culture we are applying the healing power of saving grace to its wounds and pathologies. This is a form of the prophetic ministry conferred on us through our baptismal anointing.

Now we need to decide to what extent our parish plan needs to support a prophetic ministry in today's culture. Prayer and discernment first need to determine what parts of our culture need healing. What are the negative

---

5. "A Flowering of Faith," *The Tablet* 258 (May 29, 2004), 13.

elements? Without repeating "to interpret the signs of the times," which is one of the missions of the parish (Chapter 4), we can quickly note some of the more obvious negative elements in our culture: the culture of death, secularization, relativism, individualism, materialism, militarism, consumerism, skepticism, cynicism, violence, same-sex marriage, and so on. If we are going to develop our culture we need to deal with these pathologies that afflict and shape it. Healing society's wounds with the power of saving grace is part of the development process. We, the baptized, are the Lord's instruments, or sacraments, for healing our culture.

Besides these negative elements, we need to deal with the pros and cons of postmodernism in our culture. In an interview, Tom Cruise asks: "Who's to say what's normal?" His question is a brief glimpse into postmodernism. For in the postmodern world there are no absolute norms. All truth is relative and subjective. There are no authority figures other than oneself. Besides, authority figures can no longer be trusted. It's better, for a postmodern, to celebrate difference than community. After all, everybody constructs their own privatized belief system. Thus there is no need for accountability to a community, civil or religious.[6] Postmodernism will be a tough challenge in our development of U.S. culture.

In the process of developing our culture we also need to ask what positive elements we can bless and nurture. No doubt our discernment will discover many issues our parishes will gladly cooperate with their surrounding culture, such as housing, ecumenism, education, human rights, cultural pluralism, environmental and health care issues, welcoming immigrants, and closing the gulf between the rich and the poor. (In 2004, the number of Americans living below the poverty line reached a staggering thirty-six million.)

In the past, parishes have often been inward-turning, concerned with their own pressing needs: more funds, more buildings, more volunteers, better liturgies, more sacramental ministers, paving the parking lot. Fulfilling these internal needs normally used up all the available energy and resources. Also, individual members were concerned about their own salvation. They paid little attention to building a healthy culture or earthly city within which all people could live in peace and harmony. For them,

---

6. I am indebted to Sister Donna Markham OP, PhD for her excellent handout on "Pastoral Leadership for Postmodern Times."

their religion was a private, personal matter. So they were eager to observe the "wall" between the sacred and the secular: "Let everybody mind their own religious or secular business." Finally, they were conditioned to wait for leadership "from above."

There is little doubt that presently a distinctly Catholic voice within the U.S. culture is close to non-existent. *The CARA Report* concludes that "National culture shapes individual opinions on moral issues both Catholic and non-Catholic."[7] The conclusions of the project on *American Catholics in the Public Square* go even further: "in the naked public square...not only Catholicism but all religious influence has been reduced to an extent possibly unprecedented in American history."[8] The urgent need for a prophetic voice within the U.S. culture is becoming clearer every day.

For this reason, our parishes, responding to the positive message of Vatican II's "Proper Development of Culture," will need to undergo a conversion, to turn outward, to their own secular community, to build a healthy culture for all the people. The church's official morning prayer will become their motto: "Make our work today bear fruit for our brothers and sisters— let us build with them and for them an earthly city that pleases you."

In spite of the all the examples given above, "culture" can still be a slippery word. Thus the *Pastoral Constitution on the Church in the Modern World* of Vatican II had to spell out several definitions of this term. But in a "general sense," says the constitution, "culture indicates all those factors by which man refines and unfolds his manifold spiritual and bodily qualities."[9] "Culture" writes Wilfred LaCroix, "is the human air we breathe, the human ground we tread and build on, the images we use to express ourselves and to relate to others and to our world."[10] Thus Pope John Paul II could speak of the "culture of death" when referring to abortion, euthanasia, and capital punishment.

We don't like to "rock the boat," but that's exactly what the prophets did. We know that "the holy people of God shares also in Christ's prophet-

---

7. *The CARA Report*, 9 (Winter 2004), 5.

8. Margaret O'Brien Steinfels, ed., *American Catholics, American Culture: Tradition and Resistance* (New York: Sheed and Ward, 2004), xv.

9. No. 53.

10. *Catholicism at the Millennium* (Kansas City, MO: Rockhurst University Press, 2001), 80.

ic office,"[11] including all the baptized. "Now I would like all of you to speak in tongues," writes Saint Paul, "but even more to prophesy" (1 Cor 14:5). So the future parish plan will support the cry of its prophets. Their cry may be countercultural: "Peace, not war!" "Life, not death!" "Let the poor enjoy our feast of plenty!" "Let's rescue the feast of the birthday of our Savior from the gods of commercialism!" "Let's reclaim the resurrection of the Lord from our secular Easter." "Let the laborer receive just wages!" "Let's find a home for the homeless, clothing for the naked, health care for the sick poor, and a warm welcome for the immigrants!"

Historically, institutions, civil or religious, do not easily tolerate, much less support, the prophetic voice. But silence, doing nothing, can be disastrous, both for the state and for the church. In 1994, the government of Rwanda, Africa, committed genocide, massacring 800,000 of its own citizens with knives, machetes, and grenades. Meanwhile, that country's religious leaders, with few exceptions, said and did nothing. The church's prophetic voice was silent. The smell of death persists to this day.

In the history of religion and politics the Dietrich Bonhoeffers are rare. During the Second World War, Bonhoeffer boldly confronted the Nazi menace and the "mindless Christian patriotism" in Germany: "If we claim to be Christians," he wrote, "there is no room for expediency."[12] His was a lonely prophetic voice. He is honored in death; he was persecuted in life.

In the development of our U.S. culture our parish plan will necessarily cross into the political world. The relationship between the church and politics is always delicate. "Political engagement in the parish must be approached with nuance and caution," writes Vincent Miller. But then he continues:

> Such caution, however, can quickly slide into the social convention of polite society that considers direct and specific talk about politics and religion to be impolite and polarizing…the parish can be the place in which politics can be re-grounded….In the parish, people are spurred to political action, not only by reli-

---

11. *Dogmatic Constitution on the Church*, no. 12.

12. Paul Johnson, *A History of Christianity* (New York: Atheneum, 1976), 494.

gious and ethical doctrines, but also because they belong to a particular community and become more aware of their obligations to their brothers and sisters in Christ.[13]

Churches and their parishes can be too anxious to enjoy the support of their governments, whatever the political party. They can easily be tempted to silence the prophetic voice to gain some favor or freedom from the secular powers. But Amos, the prophet, rebuked the rulers of Israel because they "commanded the prophets, saying, 'You shall not prophesy'" (2:12). The future parish will plan to recover its prophetic voice. It will be the voice for the voiceless, especially for the poor. It will discern both the positive and the negative elements in its surrounding culture.

Wouldn't it be a wonderful response to Vatican II if each parish had a committee on its parish pastoral council, entitled "The Parish Discernment Committee"? Its job description would be twofold: the prayerful discernment of the negative and positive elements in its own community's culture, and proposing a Christian response for development of that culture. Discernment, after all, is one of the gifts given to the baptized (1 Cor 12:10).

Fundamentalism

Widespread and growing fundamentalism is another of our cultural pathologies, a serious negative element, but it's difficult to define as a pathology, since there are many variations across and within the different sects of religions and within our culture. A few extremists in the various religious sects tend to define it. The parish, then, will need to do considerable discernment before it denounces any specific form. In general fundamentalism has been defined as:

> a religious way of being that manifests itself as a strategy by which beleaguered believers attempt to preserve their distinctive identity as a people or group....Catholic fundamentalism is a corruption of Catholic values, especially of sacramentality. It sees the world as evil and dangerous, forgetting that God is its Creator, Redeemer, and Sanctifier...it tends to be militant in

---

13. "Politics and the Parish," *America* 191 (August 16–23, 2004), 18–20.

style and more antagonistic to the enemies within than to those outside.[14]

"Fundamentalists" notes R. Scott Appleby, "see the world dualistically and perceive themselves to be in clash of good against evil."[15] Karen Armstrong, after reviewing the history of fundamentalism, concludes: "Fundamentalism is not going away...it is now part of the modern world."[16] She is convinced fundamentalism is rooted in fear:

> The desire to define doctrines, erect barriers, establish borders, and segregate the faithful in a sacred enclave where the law is stringently observed springs from the terror of extinction which has made all fundamentalists, at one time or another, believe that the secularists were about to wipe them out.[17]

Dualists want to be rid of the complexity of moral ambiguity. So for them, gray does not exist; everything has to be either black of white. But moral ambiguity will always remain part of our frail human condition. We remain a people composed of saints and sinners.

One effect of fundamentalism may be the new apocalyptic fear that followed the horror of 9/11 and the continuing terrorist threat. The U.S. bishops' Department of Education has rightly warned Catholics about the anti-Catholic book series *Left Behind*. These "rapture" novels exploit the dualist fundamentalism now infecting our culture. Dualism is as old and as dangerous as the heresies of Gnosticism and Manichaeism in the second and third centuries. Parish plans will include a prophetic ministry to name the false prophets of simplistic dualism and fundamentalism in our culture.[18]

The parish plan could well include the formation of a book club which, relying on modern Scripture scholars and the teaching of the church, would discuss one of the *Left Behind* novels. The purpose of the discussion would be to come to a clearer, less literal, understanding of the Scriptures.

---

14. Richard McBrien, *Catholicism* (San Francisco: HarperCollins, 1994), 94.

15. For an excellent history of fundamentalism, see Karen Armstrong, *The Battle for God* (New York: Ballantine Books, 2001).

16. Armstrong, 364, 368.

17. Armstrong, 364.

18. For more insights into methods of fundamentalism, see "God and Country," *Mother Jones*, 30 (December 2005), 9–81.

Reconciling Ministry

One can hardly watch the evening news or go to a movie without concluding that violence is another negative element in our culture. Violence is an attitude long before it emerges from the barrel of a gun. Wars and domestic, school and street violence exist as an attitude rooted in the community psyche. The assumption is that violence is the way to resolve conflict and disagreements. For this reason, parish plans will call for a permanent committee for the ministry of reconciliation and conflict partnering. Its members will serve both parish and civic communities. They will have special training through workshops and classes to develop their skills in dealing with conflict. They will be ministers of healing, reconciliation, and peacemaking in our culture, sick unto death with violence. Mohandas Gandhi will live again in every Catholic parish.

In the face of war, Christianity continues to proclaim the gospel of peace, reconciliation, and non-violence: "But if anyone strikes you on the right cheek, turn the other also" (Mt 5:39). "When you are offering your gift at the altar, if you remember that your brother or sister has something against you, leave your gift there before the altar and go; first be reconciled to your brother or sister" (Mt 5:23–24). Finally: "Blessed are the peacemakers" (Mt 5:9).

We know from history that violence breeds more violence. We also know that conflict of various kinds is the cause of violence. A committee of Conflict Partnering in every Catholic parish would be a mighty peacemaking force within our violent culture. To prepare these committees, classes or Saturday workshops taught by trained professionals could be conducted by each diocese. The Internet and most Catholic libraries provide high-quality resources for this important ministry.

Ministry of the Elderly

The average age of our population, as everyone knows, is steadily increasing. Another negative element in our culture becoming more apparent every year is the neglect of this elder population. We worship youth and hide the elderly in nursing homes. Television and movies bring us the curves of youth, not the wrinkles of old age.[19] Advertising makes its pitch

---

19. See Ram Dass, *Still Here* (New York: Riverhead Books, 2000), especially Chapter 2.

not to Grandma, but to the children of the boomers. We spend millions on cosmetic surgery to recover a youthful look, obsessed with fighting nature's normal aging process. In the meantime, our culture suffers from a growing vacuum: the wisdom of the elderly. The West could learn a lot from the cultures of the East.

But our own Western culture often rejects the cup of wisdom our seniors are eager to offer. Yet, no community, civil or religious, is self-sufficient. It needs wisdom more than hi-tech. Without wisdom the achievements of technology can be powers let loose without moral direction. Science can expand the frontiers of knowledge, loading the human brain with an infinite amount of facts and new discoveries. But if our culture lacks wisdom, these new discoveries can become dangerous playthings in the hands of children. They can turn on our culture and destroy it.

Our parish plan, therefore, will include the ministry of its elders, who may well be a font overflowing with pastoral wisdom for the parish and its surrounding culture. Moses remains a good model for the whole parish: "Moses went out to meet his father-in-law; he bowed down and kissed him" (Ex 18:7). Then he consulted the wisdom of his father-in-law and got a quick, blunt reply:

> What you are doing is not good. You will surely wear yourself out, both you and these people with you. For the task is too heavy for you; you cannot do it alone. Now listen to me. I will give you counsel, and God be with you!…You should also look for able men among all the people, men who fear God….It will be easier for you, and they will bear the burden with you. (Ex 18:17–22)

The parish plan will have a structured system for consulting its fathers-in-law, mothers-in-law, grandfathers, and grandmothers. They are a much-needed blessing to the parish in a time of great need. The parish pastoral council will gladly welcome the wisdom of the wrinkled members of the parish. Actually, the parish and society need both the new wisdom of the youth and the old wisdom of the elderly. Saint Paul does not put an age limit on the Spirit's gift of wisdom (1 Cor 12:8).

Indigenous Leadership

The parish needs a plan to discern and support its own indigenous leaders. Every genuine Christian community nurtures its own leaders. It discerns and supports the gifts of the Spirit given for the upbuilding of the community. In the early church it was the indigenous leaders of the community who became the eucharistic presiders. They earned their leadership position by hard work in the service of the community. The presbyter normally was an elder who was respected for his wisdom as a leader in his community. The early church also had its missionaries, such as Saul and Barnabas, who were sent out to Seleucia and then to Cyprus (Acts 13:4), but Paul selected indigenous leaders, like Phoebe, the deaconess, to "pastor" the church at Cenchreae.

Increased Missionary Orientation

The parish plan will have an increased missionary orientation. A team of priests, deacons, and lay ecclesial ministers will visit all the homes of the families within the parish, especially the homes of the poor. While parish ministers will continue to administer the sacraments to those who have the faith, these missionary teams will go out to those who no longer believe or never did. First, they will visit at least some of the twenty million U.S. Catholics who, for whatever reason, no longer belong to any parish. Then they will be in constant dialogue with families and schools about problems such as drugs, delinquency, hunger, the undocumented migrants, street gangs, and so on. Every parish will be a missionary outpost. Like the church of ancient Antioch, it will send its own missionaries to its own Seleucia just down the street. It will also sponsor lay missionaries to foreign lands through organizations such as the Jesuit Volunteers and the Maryknoll Lay Missionaries.

The parish plan will include a committee to welcome returning Catholics. They will be met with a warm "Welcome home!" After all, they are our brothers and sisters. Fifteen years ago, Reverend Jac Campbell, a Paulist priest in Boston, founded Landings International, a Paulist Ministry of Reconciliation with Returning Catholics. Conducted by lay volunteers, this program helps these Catholics feel at home once again and become active in their parishes. The volunteers are trained in workshops in the art of compassionate, non-judgmental listening. Each of the returnees has a unique story to tell. They get their chance during eight weekly small-group meetings that pave the way for the celebration of the sacraments of reconciliation and Eucharist. It's all part of the plan to become a more missionary parish.

Adult Faith Development

Our parish plan will emphasize adult formation and faith development. In 1884, the Third Council of Baltimore decreed that all Catholic parents were "bound to send their children to parochial schools." Ever since then, U.S. Catholic parishes have rightly spent a lot of money building and maintaining Catholic schools for their children. In the context of "godless" or "Protestant" public schools, parishes concentrated on educating their own children in the Catholic faith. While not abandoning its strong commitment to the Catholic school, the future parish will concentrate more on the education and formation of its adults. Today's changing world and culture prompt totally new questions for adults, questions that are not answered by an appeal to the catechism.

For this reason, the parish will plan to build and maintain a special "Adult Ed. Room." Carpeted, well lit, air conditioned, with excellent acoustics, it will be equipped permanently with the latest hi-tech audio and visual equipment. It will have comfortable chairs for adults (as opposed to metal folding chairs) as well as round tables for discussion. It will convert quickly from the lecture format to group discussion. It will have a library section with carrels for independent study and research. It will be equipped for Internet connection for long-distance learning of theology through linkage with the theology department of a Catholic university. Language study will also be available. Open six days and evenings in the week, it will be staffed by a competent faith formation instructor. It will be a Lifelong Learning Center.

In this center all and any questions may be asked and discussed, even if there is no answer. Adults, growing out of their early catechism answers, have doubts and many questions about their faith as taught by their first teachers. They now live in a world where everything is questioned. Science and modern cosmology confront them with questions about the old teaching about Adam and Eve as our first parents, about original sin, about redemption, and other topics. Developing adults who want to internalize a truly adult faith do not want their faith to remain dependent on the authority figures of yesteryear.

Thus our parish plan will follow through on the oft-repeated formula: "cradle to grave." The purpose of this faith formation program will be four-fold: 1. to train the growing number of lay ministers, deacons, and indigenous leaders; 2. to provide continuing education and bring adults up to date with the changing church; 3. to help adults deal with the many new challenges our modern culture and world present to an adult faith, such as cloning, stem cell research, multiculturalism, war and peace, marriage and family, same-sex marriage, parenting problems; and 4. to conduct prayerful discernment and arrive at a consensus about the parish's response to political issues and problems facing the country and the local community: poverty, pollution, drug dealing, corruption, immigration problems, moral relativism, the sex trade, binge drinking, domestic, street, and school violence. After all, through the power of the risen Lord today's disciples can heal this bent and broken world, but first they have to really believe in the power of the resurrection and develop an adult faith.

This Adult Ed. Room will have its own Web site. It will be updated weekly with a Catholic response to current events within the parish, the church, and the world. The Web site will have a chat room with questions and answers for anyone connected to the Internet. The director of this room will respond to all questions posted on the Web site, providing additional resource materials when needed.

Funding and staffing this ideal program will, of course, be a big problem for a single parish. On the other hand, with careful planning, at least one such program could be supported and made available to all parishes in each deanery or vicariate. One member of each parish pastoral council in the vicariate could form its governing council. This council would contract for staff and develop the policy for all its programs and activities.

New Language and Imagination for a New Worldview

In the revised *Catechism of the Catholic Church* (1994) we changed "Holy Ghost" to "Holy Spirit." A new name for the third person of the Blessed Trinity! It meant a change in the sign of the cross we learned in the *Baltimore Catechism*. The change caused no Catholic outcry, no protests. The words changed; the dogma did not. "Spirit" to express the divine was a good fit in our modern culture; "Ghost" was not. In the same way, the future parish will review its church language to find out if it still communicates with our modern worldview.

In the new Adult Ed. Room the parish will keep testing its church language. Does it still communicate God's love and good news to modern ears? What do the following words, taken from the *Catholic Catechism*, actually communicate today: transubstantiation, salvation, supernatural, anaphora, presbyteral, Old Covenant, Immaculate Conception, Lamb of God? How does the literal retelling of the creation story in Genesis 3 come across to modern students? They know that the universe as we know it today gradually came into existence over a span of fifteen billion years. They know that life forms developed over a period of millions of years. Human life was last in this long series of millions of years of development. Students learn all this from the Discovery Channel or any encyclopedia in any library.

Today's parishes can no longer rely on those in authority to simply repeat truth formulations that lack credibility today. They will not teach what eventually will need to be untaught. They will rely more on modern Scripture scholars to teach the power of myth, story, and symbol in leading adults into the mysteries of creation. God is not bound by earth time, nor is the infinite God defined by the poor finite words and symbols of earthlings. If our faith remains cast in the static philosophical framework of the Council of Trent (1545–63), it will not connect with the modern, evolving world.

During the Council of Nicaea (325) the church struggled with the different meanings of Greek philosophical language. The church had to find a language that would deal with the heresy of Arianism. At the same time, it had to preserve the truths of revelation as revealed in the Scriptures. It was a difficult but very necessary challenge. The church had to reconceptualize and rearticulate the faith in new symbols and formulations so it could be internalized by a different culture. The very survival of the church was at stake.

The parish today must continue to search for the right words and symbols to actually engage the present, modern world. Reconceptualizing and rearticulating the faith is an ongoing process in the development of adult faith. Being orthodox is fine, but repeating dead formulas does not proclaim the word of life. The parish's words of life must touch modern hearts, including the hearts of the rest of world.

Really connecting with the daily lives of adult Catholics today is a difficult challenge. Michael Morwood, an Australian theologian, is grappling with that challenge:

> [I]t is clear today that many Christians, in the normal process of adult faith development, are asking questions. They are disturbed that the faith they were taught rests so strongly on underlying premises people at the beginning of the twenty-first century find hard to accept. They find the language and concepts of the Nicaean Creed irrelevant to their lives. They are committed Christians, but want their faith articulated and expressed in concepts and language which respect the realities of these times.[20]

Augustine (d. 430), relying on Plato, and Thomas Aquinas (d. 1274), relying on Aristotle, rearticulated the Catholic faith for their own generations. Because of their great work our faith took on a more philosophical turn. It relied more on the language of reason than the language of the heart. But this new language at that time effectively taught the faith to people with a new worldview. This kind of work needs to be done over and over throughout history.

But rearticulation of the faith is not simply a question of replacing an old proposition or word, with a new one, such as "Spirit" for "Ghost." The new articulation must reconnect with today's unique human story. A new articulation will not be received as a saving story unless the story of Jesus includes and responds to today's human story. Every culture, every generation is the bearer of its own story. Those who embark on a new articulation of the faith must first listen with awe and reverence to their people's

---

20. *Is Jesus God?* (New York: Crossroad Publishing Co., 2001), 66.

own story, which, along with the story of evolving creation, is part of God's own story now unfolding in earth time. Thus any new articulation needs to be responsive to the differences in age, race, culture, and gender. Each difference represents a unique human story. There is no better place to begin the listening process than in the modern parish where all these different people actually live.

Common Priesthood of the Faithful

In 2003, there were 35,448 lay ecclesial ministry students in the United States. As many as 496 parishes were administered by a sister, layperson, or permanent deacon. In 2004, the number of priestless parishes in the U.S. rose to 3,157. At the same time, the number of Catholics increased from 57.4 million in 1995 to 64.3 million in 2004.

These statistics clearly point to the need for a larger role for the priesthood of the faithful in the teaching, governing, and sanctifying mission of the future parish. Vatican II was clear enough: "The baptized, by regeneration and the anointing of the Holy Spirit, are consecrated into a spiritual house and a holy priesthood."[21] All the baptized participate in the one priesthood of Christ.

Since the Council of Trent, Catholic theology at the parish level has been dominated by the ontology of difference. Priests, in virtue of their ordination, became ontologically different from the non-ordained laity. Being, permanence, and state of life became more important than function, competence, or ministry. Thus the priest was "a priest forever," even if he never performed any priestly functions. "Being a priest" was his full identity. This distinguished and separated him from the lay state. Functional competence was not the first priority in his identity. But in 1 Corinthians 12 we see an emphasis on function, on ministry, not on state of life. Thus lay persons, through their baptismal anointing into the common priesthood, can receive the Spirit's gifts to function as teachers, healers, helpers, and governors no matter their gender or state of life.

Our parish plan would emphasize gift, function, and competence over state of life. Urgent pastoral need will move theology into a more pastoral

---

21. *Dogmatic Constitution on the Church*, no. 10.

direction. Differences and variety in the ministry, both ontological and functional, will remain. While we honor variety, we also need order in the ministries. But the common priesthood of the faithful, conferred by the baptismal anointing, will blossom into a variety of new forms to build up the future parish. The burning question will not be, "How different are we from one another?" But, "What do we have in common?" Answer: the common priesthood of the faithful. Our modern culture is more impressed by competence in the actual ministry than by differences in rank and states of life. We can't divide the one priesthood of Christ into two priesthoods, one for the laity and one for the ordained. Parish plans will be the visible sign that the one priesthood of Christ can, and does, operate in a variety of forms.

As Christians, we do not passively await whatever the future brings. Rather, humbly relying on guidance of the Spirit, we go out as the Lord's anointed disciples with a common vision to build and plan our community's future. That's our vocation as faithful ministers to the kingdom of God. "Then I saw a new heaven and a new earth; for the first heaven and the first earth had passed away....They need no light of lamp or sun, for the Lord God will be their light" (Rev 21:1, 22:5).

For Reflection and Discussion

1. Which of these proposals for a parish plan would you like to see implemented in your parish?

2. Which proposal do you like the most? Which one do you like the least?

2. What obstacles do you foresee in starting a "Parish Discernment Committee" for the development of the U.S. culture in your community?

3. How will you evaluate progress with your parish plan?

4. Does the thought of a prophetic ministry make you nervous? Why or why not?

5. Do you see any priorities for your parish in the proposed plan? Which part of the plan would you implement first, second, third?

PART II

Select Issues Concerning the Administration of a Parish in Canon Law

John S. Weber

Introduction

This section deals with canon law as it relates to the definition of a parish and its consequences on membership, rights, and obligations of the faithful in their various vocational roles, and the basic structures of a parish administration and how it deals with money and property. This section does not deal with the most life-giving dimensions of parish life: liturgy, sacraments, preaching, social outreach. The church as corporation must deal with federal, state, and church laws. "The church is not a democracy" is often heard. In many ways it is more a feudal structure with "layered monarchies": pope, bishop, pastor, parish secretary and the Director of Religious Education. Each has a smaller kingdom but often exercises absolute discretionary power in their individual domains. This has become a problem, with each level not knowing their canonical or civil law limits. At the risk of becoming legalistic, one must understand structures and the various kinds of power and influence in decision making. Clearly one must understand the limits they work within. Better understanding of the basics can lead to more mutual respect and harmony between bishops and pastors and between pastors and their financial councils and parish councils.

CHAPTER 6

The Parish in Canon Law

What Is a Parish?

According to canon law, a parish "is a certain community of the Christian faithful stably constituted in a particular church, whose pastoral care is entrusted to a pastor as its proper pastor under the authority of the diocesan bishop" (canon 515, §1). There are three elements here: a certain community of Christian faithful, a particular church, and a proper pastor.

You can define that "certain community" is two ways: geographically or personally (canon 518). A geographic parish—the vast majority—has physical boundaries. Every Catholic living within those boundaries belongs to that parish. It is irrelevant to the law (but not to pastor!) that you are registered or use envelopes or even show up. You belong. Geography and baptism give you rights in a parish.

The other way of defining that "certain community" is personally. It does not matter where you live (no boundaries on a map) as long as you fulfill the criteria for belonging to the parish as they have been defined in its decree of establishment. The most typical examples of this kind of parish are defined either by language or ethnic heritage (the Spanish-speaking parish) or by membership in some group or institution, such as a university parish or the military/diplomatic parish.

Pastors and Their Duties

Ideally, every parish must have a pastor who is a priest (canon 521). And again, ideally, there must be only one pastor per parish and one parish per pastor. There are exceptions and modifications. The "pastor must possess stability [of place] and therefore is to be appointed for an indefinite period of time. The diocesan bishop can appoint him only for a specific period if the conference of bishops has permitted this by a decree" (canon 522). Most pastors in this country are appointed for a term which the Vatican has decreed must be six years. A pastor can be reappointed to multiple six-year terms at the will of the bishop. To remove and/or transfer a pastor during his term or during his indefinite tenure, the bishop must use the canons at the end of the code if the pastor does not agree to it. The law presumes that the pastor provides a permanent presence and a sense of continuity for the community.

The pastor (and especially the bishop) has an impossible job description. Several canons define his duties. Canon 528 requires pastors to make sure that the word of God is proclaimed in its entirety; instructs in the truths of the faith; gives a homily on all Sundays and holy days of obligation; gives catechetical instructions; fosters works inspired by the gospel and social justice; cares for the Catholic education of children and youth; and evangelizes the lapsed Catholics and the unchurched. He is to foster the Eucharist and penance and the other sacraments; have family prayers; participate in the liturgy; and prevent abuses. Canon 529 states that the pastor is to know his people; visit families; share in their cares, anxieties, and griefs; strengthen them and correct them; help the sick and dying; seek out the poor, the afflicted, the lonely, those exiled from their home country, others weighed down by special difficulties; and to help spouses and parents. The pastor is also to recognize and promote the laity in their proper mission of the church; foster their associations for the purpose of religion; cooperate with the bishop and the other priests of the diocese; and help the laity see beyond their parish and be active members of a diocese and the universal church.

The following tasks are especially entrusted to the pastor: the administration of baptism, of confirmation in danger of death, of Viaticum and anointing of the sick, of the apostolic blessing, of marriage and nuptial blessings, of funeral rites, of blessing baptismal font at Easter; and to preside over processions outside the church, solemn blessings outside the church, and the more solemn eucharistic celebration on Sundays and holy days of obligation.

Canon 532 refers to the pastor as the sole representative of the parish in legal and financial affairs. As such, he is to see that canons 1281–88 are observed. These are dealt with in detail in Chapter 8, "Parish Governance," which deals with the section on administration of goods in Book V of the code.

A pastor generally is required to reside in a rectory near the church. Each year he gets one month vacation and a spiritual retreat (canon 533). He is required to "apply a Mass for the people entrusted to him on each Sunday and holy day of obligation in his diocese" (canon 534).

He is to keep accurate sacramental registers for baptism, marriage, and death. He is to oversee the parish seal and archives (canon 535). He is to preside over the parish pastoral council (536, §1) and be assisted by the finance council (canon 537).

A pastor can resign but it must be accepted by the bishop for validity. At age seventy-five, the pastor is requested by canon law to resign (canon 538); but again it must be accepted by the bishop in order to take effect.

The net effect of his having to be "all things to all people" is that the pastor cannot do it all. Even in very small, rural parishes with relatively limited demands, the pastor himself is still limited by his own talents and deficits. This enables and pressures the pastor to encourage the laity to fulfill their mission in the church. The problem is that many of the roles of the laity in the church are functionally defined by the limitations of the pastor. These limitations may be linguistic, geographic, scheduling, health, lack of interest, energy, knowledge, or talent. People then fill the gaps either as volunteers or as employees. This can work well with the pastor and his helpers becoming a well integrated and effective team.

When there is a change of pastors, though, everyone's tenure is questionable. The new priest who might be much more personally invested in issues dealing with the physical plant or finances or liturgy or teaching youth or marriage preparation may well simply dismiss the people previously performing these tasks and create a lot of ill will. The same is true for the bishop on the diocesan scale. The pastor has the right and the duty to see to all these functions and he can do it "his way."

Beyond these "task" issues, there are personality issues. This is a recipe for chaos among lay employees over the long haul. They do not have the comparable rights, protections, and guarantees as employees as the pastor does in his role as pastor. There is only a call to fulfill the mission of the church, but no balance between the rights, duties, and obligations between the clergy and the laity in accomplishing this. The right to organize into church worker labor unions is not warmly received. Currently, the laity fill in the gaps of their pastor.

Domicile, or "Canonical Residency"

The defining canon (canon 515) on parishes mentions a "proper pastor." The proper pastor is where the layperson has either "domicile" or "quasi-domicile." "Domicile is acquired by that residence within the territory of a certain parish...which either is joined with the intention of remaining there permanently or has been protracted for five complete years" (canon 102, §1). On the other hand, "quasi-domicile is acquired by residence within the territory of a certain parish...which either is joined with the intention of remaining there for at least three months unless called away or has in fact been protracted for three months"(canon 102, §2). Both domicile and quasi-domicile are obtained immediately upon arrival if the intention to stay the required time is present. It is "through both domicile and quasi-domicile [that] each person acquires his or her pastor." Parishioners can demand or vindicate their rights only with their proper pastor. This becomes important at times of baptisms, first confession and communion, weddings and funerals (though canon 1177 allows for some exceptions for funerals).

These rights are acquired for personal parishes if the person falls within the population defined in the establishment of the personal parish. Being a student, faculty member, or staff member of the university would qualify for university parishes generally. Speaking the language of the group for whom a parish was established (for instance, Spanish, Vietnamese) would qualify one as a member with domicile—if the time requirements or intention were fulfilled.

Parish Registration

What is parish registration then? This concept is not in the Code of Canon Law. It can be merely a census of those living in the territory or belonging to an authorized group in personal parishes. Registration does not make a person a member. It is only a list. Living in the territory of a territorial parish and/or belonging to the authorized group for which the personal parish was founded is the only criterion. By custom (which can develop into the force of law in certain circumstances) registration might become a new criterion in this country. But it hasn't yet. If someone registers in another parish or use another parish's envelopes, then a psychological or financial connection with that parish is developed. One may, in fact, exercise all spiritual needs there, but it is by way of favor of the pastor or by custom. By so doing, the rights in the canonical or proper parish are not revoked.

Basic Rights of Parishioners

One does not have to register, use envelopes, or even attend in order to acquire these rights. The law grants them directly. One just has to be a baptized Catholic who lives within the boundaries of a territorial parish or a member of the designated group of a personal parish. Among the various lists of rights and obligations are the following: the right to make known one's needs (especially spiritually) and desires (canon 212, §2); the right and duty to tell the sacred pastors (bishops) and everyone else one's opinion on anything regarding the good of the church (canon 212, §3); the right to receive assistance out of the spiritual goods of the church, especially the word of God and the sacraments (canon 213); the right to worship God and follow one's own form of spiritual life (canon 214); the right to establish and direct associations for charity, piety (canon 215), or apostolic action (216); the right to a Christian education (canon 217); the right to study the sacred subjects (Bible, theology, canon law); the right to be free from any kind of coercion in choosing a state in life (canon 219); the right to privacy and a good reputation (canon 220); the right to vindicate and defend one's rights (canon 221, §1); the right not to be punished by canonical penalties except according to the norm of law (canon 221, §3); the right of parents to educate their children (canon 226, §2). These are more fully developed in Chapter 7: "Rights and Obligations in Canon Law."

Practical issues stemming from these principles include the fact that the pastor cannot refuse parents to baptize their child because they don't use envelopes or are not registered. Parishioners have a right to form groups in the parish in order to lobby for and practice various spiritualities—even if the pastor does not like those particular expressions of Catholicism. But he does not have to be there with them. Nor can a parishioner be punished by the pastor or the bishop except according to the law.

All of these are underdeveloped in the current jurisprudence. Everyone has heard the saying that "the church is not a democracy." That's true. But there is only one Roman Pontiff in the world and only one proper ordinary in the diocese and only one proper pastor in the parish. Even though "as successors of the apostles, bishops automatically enjoy in the dioceses entrust to them all the ordinary, proper and immediate authority required for the exercise of their pastoral office,"[1] they are not the pope. The pastor is not the bishop. The parish secretary or the director of religious education is not the pastor. Everywhere, it seems that someone is claiming that "ordinary, proper and immediate authority" in their particular baliwick. Bishops, priests, administrators of all kinds can and do trample upon the rights of the laity on occasion. But the church purports to be a visible establishment of the kingdom of God. This kingdom of love and charity is bolstered by a system of laws. Ignored and unknown rights are useless. The next chapter hopes to shed light on these rights.

For Reflection and Discussion

1. Are we helped or hurt by the fact that "the buck stops with the pastor"? Explain.

2. Does the pastor foster unity in your parish?

3. Can there be "tenure" or job security in church employment?

4. How can divisions within a parish be addressed?

5. How do you feel about the resident baptized Catholic who is not registered but demands his rights?

---

1. *Decree on the Pastoral Office of Bishops in the Church*, 8.

CHAPTER 7

Rights and Obligations in Canon Law

The 1983 Code of Canon Law has the church's first "bill of rights." In fact, there are four of them! The first list (canons 208–23) deals with the obligations and rights of all Christian faithful. These belong to the baptized in general. Then there are three more specific lists relating to the three major groups of baptized people: the laity, clergy, and the religious. Canons 224–31 deal with the obligations and rights of the laity. The list that deals with the obligations and rights of clerics is found in canons 273–89. The list for the religious is found in canons 662–72. Here we will deal with the first two lists only, all the baptized and the laity. The obligations and rights of clerics and religious do not directly affect the parish as much. The obligations and rights of pastors were considered earlier.

One begins to suspect that calling them a "bill of rights" may be too optimistic. The two titles of these lists, "The Obligations and Rights of…" tend to emphasize the obligations, but a few good nuggets are there as well. With aggressive development of canonical jurisprudence, these rights can become powerful factors in the future life of the church. It is the first list (the one for anyone baptized) that is the most inclusive and applicable to everyone.

The Obligations and Rights of All Christians

The first list deals with the obligations and rights of every baptized person, regardless of whether they are single or married lay people, ordained as a deacon, priest, or bishop, or a religious man or woman in public vows. (Note that a religious can be either male or female, and a male religious can be either clerical or lay depending on whether or not he is also ordained.) A professed, ordained male would be subject to three lists: all the baptized, the clergy, and the religious. A professed female could not be ordained but is subject to three lists as well: the ones relating to the baptized, the laity, and the religious, but not the clergy. At its root, the church is divided into two groups of people: clerics and laity. Religious orders, societies, and congregations form "a third thing" in the church. Secular institutes give us a new confounding factor. Non-canonical groups have become more popular in the last thirty years. They are by definition outside the scope of canon law of religious but do fall under the rubrics of the Christian faithful (all baptized) and the laity.

The canons concerning personal status can seem confusing, but the Christian faithful come in a wide variety of situations. This first list covers all of us—if we are baptized.

Equality

Baptism is the foundational reality here. From baptism flows "a true equality regarding dignity and action by which they all cooperate in the building up of the body of Christ according to each one's own condition and function" (canon 208). This canon emphasizes the equality of dignity and worth of everyone who is baptized. There are many different conditions and functions that need to be coordinated in building up the church. These include male or female, married or single, parent or child, religious and/or cleric (bishop, priest, deacon). These differences can be valued differently by different people, but in the eyes of God, all are equal. They are different vocations having differing jobs and responsibilities in the body of Christ. As Paul emphasizes, all gifts and talents are for building up the body of Christ; they are not to be a source of pride, but a responsibility to share. The more one has, the more will be demanded.

Universal and Particular Churches

From this flows the obligation to maintain communion with the church and to fulfill duties to both the universal church and the particular church (canon 209). The "particular church" is generally understood to be the diocese, the basic church. The "universal church" is the abstraction of all the particular churches in communion with each other. To use an American analogy, there has always been a "federalist versus states' rights" struggle in the church. Historians frequently say that the Civil War changed our country from being "the states united" to "the united states." It's a matter of emphasis and identity. The diocese is the church we belong to and live in. The diocese is united with all others forming the universal church. The diocese of Rome is not the universal church, but another particular church. Its bishop, the bishop of Rome, also happens to be the Primate of Italy, the Patriarch of the West, the successor to the Apostles Peter and Paul, the vicar of Peter in the first millennium and, after the First Lateran Council (1123), the Vicar of Christ in the second millennium. We simply call him the pope.

These unity and communion issues also exist on the smaller scale within a diocese. Parishes need to show their solidarity with the broader diocese and the broader church. On the lay level this is often done with money—fund raising and taxes for the support of the diocese and second collections for the support of national issues (for example, minorities, Catholic communication, home missions) or international issues (foreign missions or for the pope himself, Peter's Pence). But solidarity is also needed on the personal level, an individual's time and talents and not just finances. Parishioners are needed to serve on diocesan boards and committees and even at times on national committees and at national or international gatherings. All of these forge communion and identity on the various levels of church—from the domestic church, which is the family, to the parish church, to the diocesan church, to the national level of church, to the universal church.

There are various people who perform "hinge" or "bridge" functions between these various levels. "Cardinal" (hinge) and "Pontifex" (bridge-builder) are the two terms most associated with these two functions, but they also serve at all levels of church. The pastor is the hinge and the bridge between the people of his parish and the people of the diocese as a whole. The bishop is the hinge and the bridge between his people and the people of the larger church. Each level contains within its job description the call to meet the needs within its boundaries and to build links of communion with the church beyond itself. The environmental bumper sticker, "Think Globally, Act Locally" applies here. The church, like the environment, acts on the largest and the smallest scales.

Continual Sanctification

"All the Christian faithful must direct their efforts to lead a holy life and to promote the growth of the church and its continual sanctification, according to their own condition" (canon 210). This is a generic "do good and avoid evil" canon that says everything in general but nothing in particular at the same time. The phrase, "according to their own condition," indicates that the different states and circumstances within the church carry different opportunities and responsibilities. All are called to worship in the liturgy, but many differing roles express this canon in myriad complementary ways. Presiders preside; preachers preach; choirs sing; acolytes serve; ushers help; all pray and are fed by word and sacrament.

Different vocations call for different, even mutually exclusive, behaviors. Celibates are chaste by sublimating their sexual energies into ministry, while spouses are chaste by praising God in a healthy, life-giving, active sex life. Priests take the place of Christ—"*in persona Christi*"—while spouses take the place of God the Creator in their role as "pro-creators" in procreation.

The kingdom of God is built and maintained by thousands of functions, each done well and each important to the whole. Each is to be motivated by the Spirit, following the example of Jesus and done in praise and honor of the Father.

Evangelization: "Being" and "Spreading" the Good News

"All the Christian faithful have the duty and right to work so that the divine message of salvation more and more reaches all people in every age and in every land" (canon 211). All the baptized are to live the gospel effectively according to their times and circumstances in such a way that people will see how they love one another. As Francis of Assisi once observed, "Preach the gospel at all times, and when necessary, use words." Behavior proclaims more effectively and eloquently than words.

Obedience, Needs, and Desires

With three qualifications, Christians "are bound to follow…those things which the sacred pastors…declare as teachers of the faith or establish as rulers of the church" (canon 212, §1). Before examining the qualifications, the core statement needs some explication.

Who are these Christians, or more precisely, "the Christian faithful," as the canon states? Previous canons modify this. "The canons of this Code regard only the Latin Church" (canon 1). This means that persons who do not belong to the Latin Church (or more commonly known as the Roman Catholic Church, or the Roman Rite) are not bound to this code. The code sometimes has canons that reflect what theology calls "natural law" and "divine law." When certain canons are based on natural law or divine law, then they bind everyone because according to the church everyone is bound by natural law and divine law. Inclusion in the Code of Canon Law does not add to their binding power; it merely reiterates it. In general, "*merely ecclesiastical* laws bind those who have been baptized in the Catholic Church…possess sufficient use of reason…and have completed seven years of age" (canon 11). So, a person who is not baptized in the Latin Rite, or is not sufficiently cognitively developed, or is not yet seven years old, does not have to obey.

Who are "sacred pastors"? Does a particularly pious pastor who wears a black cassock and reads his breviary in church before liturgy qualify as a sacred pastor? No. "Sacred pastors" is a term reserved for bishops. "Sacred ministers" is used in canons 207 and 1008. It refers to clerics in general—bishops, priests, and deacons—who are distinguished from "ministers" such as lectors, acolytes, eucharistic ministers, ministers of charity, and the like. "Sacred pastors" can refer to the college of bishops in its entirety or to an individual bishop for his diocese. It distinguishes "pastors" of parishes who must be priests from bishops who are pastors of the diocese or the pope who is sometimes referred as the Supreme Pastor. It does not distinguish between holy and unholy pastors.

"Declare as teachers" and "establish as rulers" cover quite a bit. There are no bright red lines limiting exactly what these two terms cover. They are deliberately broad, extensive, and inclusive. This gives the benefit of the doubt to the bishops' directions. Clearly, though, it does not include anything contrary to law, contrary to morals and those instances that are merely personal expressions of selfishness, immaturity, and self-aggrandizement.

So, given that Christians are bound to obey, what are the necessary qualifications to promote obedience? There are three. The first is "conscious of their own responsibility"; the second is "to follow with Christian obedience"; and the third is "inasmuch as they represent Christ."

The first qualification, "conscious of their own responsibility," refers to someone's particular personal status in the church. First and foremost it refers to baptism and then to anything that qualifies or directs how one lives the baptismal life (being married, being single, being a cleric). Being a spouse and a parent highlights different functions in the body of Christ than being a pastor of a parish or a bishop of a diocese. Through the prism of baptism all are equal in the eyes of God, but everyone is not equally responsible for everything in the church.

The second qualification for every baptized person is "to follow with Christian obedience." Is Christian obedience different from military obedience or the obedience of a child due to a parent or of an employee to an employer?

Many people have a military model in mind when they think of obedience. This model emphasizes unquestioning, immediate, reflexive obedience. This is most useful in battle when an officer needs to order someone to do something that is likely to result in death. Generally, the commanding sacred pastor does not require this type of obedience (not even in the Crusades!).

Others have in mind the family model of obedience. Granted that there may be times when the sacred pastor feels like he is dealing with a three year old, this model denigrates the adult dignity of any non-bishop member of the church. Adults need to be treated as adults. Human maturity and health is a requirement for a holy church. Perfection, holiness, is the goal of all obedience, but human maturity is a requirement. Presuming immaturity and acting paternalistically leads to dysfunctional church.

Nor is the employee/employer model appropriate for the church. We are not trading our time and efforts for a paycheck, neither from the bishop nor from God! We do not earn our way to heaven. Salvation is not a benefit in lieu of wages, but a free gift from God. It's a demanding gift, but still a gift. Our job is not to earn salvation, but to accept it and be grateful. We are not to be the hirelings who guard the sheep but run away at the first sign of a wolf. We are, rather, sons and daughters of the Most High. Our commitment is in our life, not in our paycheck. So, we are not to obey just because that's what we are paid to do, because "that's what I hired you to do."

Christian obedience, then, is the obedience Jesus had in doing the will of his Father. That is, at the same time, more demanding and more nebulous than any of the models above.

The second section of canon 212 deals with the right of all the Christian faithful (lay and clergy alike) to approach the pastors (parish pastors, diocesan pastors, and the universal pastor) with "their needs, especially spiritual ones, and their desires." This canon guarantees that the lines of communication between the leaders and members of the church are open. Dialogue certainly does not guarantee that petitioners will get their way, but it does guarantee that they are heard. Being ignored leads to alienation, which goes against the fabric of the people of God.

The third section of canon 212 builds on the previous right of communication and turns it into the qualified "duty to manifest to the sacred pastors (bishops) their opinion on matters which pertain to the good of the church and to make their opinion known to the rest of the church faithful." This duty is qualified in several ways. The person should have knowledge, competence, and prestige regarding the issue involved. It might be theologians regarding theology, musicians regarding liturgy, accountants or finance mangers regarding money, educators regarding religious education, or parents regarding their children. The only limitations are that it should not warp, prejudice, or do harm to the integrity of faith or morals. It should promote the common advantage (the common good) and the dignity of persons. It also must be respectful of the pastors involved.

Right to Spiritual Goods

"The Christian faithful have the right to receive assistance from the sacred pastors out of the spiritual goods of the church, especially the world of God and the sacraments" (canon 213). Here "spiritual goods" is distinguished from "temporal goods." "Goods" is not a word we use very often.

"You got the goods?" means "Do you have the items or things?" This has been frequently heard in legally suspect situations, such as after a robbery. Theoretically we could use the word "bads" too, but we don't because we are dealing with positive things related to the spiritual life. In a later chapter we deal with "temporal goods" (as opposed to eternal goods, ultimately, eternal life), which basically refers to money and the administration of worldly goods (property).

Spiritual goods is a very broad category including anything that is helpful in the life of the Holy Spirit working in us. As the canon points out, it especially highlights the word of God and the sacraments. But it includes many other things such as the "deposit of faith," other religious truth and teachings, devotions, blessings, rituals, indulgences, processions, and whatever the religious culture needs and treasures.

The Christian faithful (both laity and clerics) have this right to receive assistance from the sacred pastors (bishops). The burden is placed on the bishops to assist and provide for the spiritual quest for everyone in his diocese and to have solicitude for and to collaborate with all the other bishops for the universal church.

The most immediate and practical expression of this canon is that all of us have a right to the sacraments. Baptism, first confession, first communion, anointing of the sick, confirmation, and marriage cannot be refused except for a proportionally weighty reason. "Especially the sacraments" adds weight to its presumption of availability. The specific canons on each of these sacraments limit and narrow this broad right in Book IV: The Sanctifying Function of the Church. Also, canon 223 mandates a balancing act of "the common good of the church, the rights of others and their own duties toward others" as well as "ecclesiastical authority can direct the exercise of rights which are proper to the Christian faithful." There is a complicated calculus involved here. One cannot simply demand the sacraments in light of canon 213 to the exclusion of all other considerations.

Access to the word of God is also especially mandated by canon 213. This includes both good preaching and Bible study. The mysteries, the histories, and the developments of the various parts of the Bible are generally unknown. Wrestling with the red meat of the Bible is ultimately much more rewarding than spinning designs out of the cotton candy of many popular devotions and distractions! Cotton candy is pretty and sweet, but one would die of malnutrition if that is all one eats!

Having said this, and having emphasized the primacy of word and sacrament, the next canon describes the right of each individual to worship according to his rite (Latin Rite for most of us in this country) and the right of everyone "to follow their own form of spiritual life so long as it is consonant with the doctrine of the church" (canon 214).

There are many rites in the church. The Latin Rite is the most familiar one to most Westerners. The Byzantine Rite and the Maronite Rite are other fairly common rites of the universal church. There are several others currently and historically, many of which are quite exotic and highly localized. They are some of the broad strokes of universality in the church.

The various schools of spirituality, the various devotions, practices, and customs give color and texture to the various local churches and individuals in the universal church. Just as each individual is different biologically and socially, so each individual is uniquely spiritual. No one approach fits all at any one time or over time. Yet, not all ideas, not all variations, not all customs, and not all innovations are good. The canon warns that everything must be "consonant with the doctrine of the church."

The next canon is the "free association" canon of the code. "The Christian faithful are at liberty freely to found and direct associations for purposes of charity or piety or for the promotion of the Christian vocation in the world and to hold meetings for the common pursuit of these purposes" (canon 215). There are no qualifiers in this particular canon, unlike the previous one on being "consonant with the doctrine of the church." There are several groups of committed Catholics who meet to discuss and defend proposals that go against church doctrines or at least against church policies. Ultimately, it is up the to the diocesan bishop to lead, decree, and legislate for his diocese regarding groups deemed unacceptable. Not all bishops view things the same way, so there are many discrepancies between dioceses. This is all part of the fabric of universality. Unity is not conformity. Reasonable people do disagree. Time is often the best prerequisite to smoothing out the various "wrinkles" in the church fabric.

In summary, this list of rights and obligations is new to the code. Previously, such rights were expressed in a left-handed way—duties of the pastors to their flocks. Now they are listed (canonized) in the code as consequences of the sacrament of baptism and located in each individual. Many proposals and controversies swirled about the church in this first attempt at a "bill of rights." It is a very fertile ground for future jurisprudence in balancing all of the obligations and rights of the many members of the people of God.

The Obligations and Rights of All Lay Christians

This second title of obligations and rights deals specifically with one group of the baptized, the largest group: the laity. This title specifies and refines the general obligations and rights listed above. Rather than dealing with each canon, only the pertinent points will be addressed here.

Secular Sphere

Canon 225 builds on the more general duty of all the baptized "to be" and "to do" the good news (the gospel) "in the world." The church recognizes two spheres: the secular and the religious. Those who are ordained or in the vowed state of being a member of a religious order or a secular institute generally are called to working in the religious sphere. Those who are single lay people or married lay people work primarily in the secular sphere. "[T]he divine message is [to be] made known and accepted by all persons everywhere in the world. This obligation is even more compelling in those circumstances in which only through them can people hear the gospel and know Christ" (canon 225, §1). This refers to the workplace, civil society as a whole, unions, schools, politics, and other places where one would not ordinarily find clergy or religious. All laity are "bound by a particular duty to imbue and perfect the order of temporal affairs with the spirit of the gospel and thus to give witness to Christ, especially in carrying out these same affairs and in exercising secular functions" (canon 225, §2). This canon directly flows from the *Decree on the Apostolate of Lay People* of the Second Vatican Council, where there was a great debate about the apostolate. Prior to the council, the apostolate was the sphere of the hierarchy. The council decreed that the apostolate is exercised by all the baptized.

Marriage

In the Latin Church, marriage is generally not an option for the clergy or for religious. Only lay people can be married. Marriage is the vocational sacrament for the laity and they are "to build up the people of God" (canon 226, §1).

The education of their children is "a most grave obligation and [they] possess the right to educate them" (canon 226, §2). This right is so great that the state is also bound to help parents in this regard. "Parents must possess a true freedom in choosing schools; therefore, the Christian faithful must be concerned that civil society recognizes this freedom for parents and even supports it with subsidies; distributive justice is to be observed" (canon 797). These canons encourage parents to be politically involved so that Catholic parents not only have the right to choose a school for their children, but that they must also be politically involved so that the state even subsidizes it to a "just" degree. This canon has obviously implications for the Catholic school system and the church's view that the state must support Catholic schools according to the norms of distributive justice, (which means that all the resources and opportunities of the state are distributed equitably among all its citizens). This is one instance where the Catholic Church claims support for a church project (education). The interpretation of the two religion clauses of the First Ammendment causes unique problems for the United States, which Canada and many European countries do not share.

Civil Freedoms

Canon 227 states that "all the laity have the right to have recognized that freedom which all citizens have in the affairs of the earthly city." So the state cannot infringe on a Catholic's rights because of religion. Again, the global reach of this canon reflects the church's concern about totalitarian states infringing on Catholics' freedoms. Yet, at the same time, Catholics cannot make use of such freedoms or rights that go against the gospel or the church's magisterium. Many Western democracies have civil freedoms that the church condemns.

Lay Ministry

Canon 228 has two sections dealing with ecclesiastical offices and functions. No right to these positions is expressed, but the principle that "suitable and qualified" persons "are able to exercise [these offices and functions] according to the precepts of the law." They can also "be experts and advisors, even in councils, according to the norm of law." Many jobs in the church used to be staffed by priests and religious. As the Vatican Council II decreed, baptism and confirmation make everyone qualified for the apostolate within the church as well as in the world. This canon basically empowers bishops and priests to build up the church by using the expertise and talents of the laity. Lectors, acolytes, communion ministry, and membership on the diocesan and parish finance and pastoral councils are just the beginning.

Religious Education

The first section of canon 229 is a strongly worded canon declaring that

> lay persons are bound by the obligation and possess the right to acquire knowledge of Christian doctrine appropriate to the capacity and condition of each in order for them to be able to live according to this doctrine, announce it themselves, defend it if necessary, and take their part in exercising the apostolate.

To live, to explain, to defend our faith and traditions require knowledge. This again is an expression and a precondition for lay people being active in the apostolate of the church, which was a major theme of the Vatican Council II.

The second section deals with the most formal aspect of this need for knowledge, enrolling in ecclesiastical institutions of higher learning and continuing education and formation in the faith. The third section deals with the qualification of the laity to receive the ecclesiastical mandate given by the bishop to teach the sacred sciences in his diocese, which is required of all professors in higher education. Generally these functions were reserved to the clergy. Now they are available to qualified lay persons.

This whole canon is a particular application of the more general principle enunciated in canon 211.

Ministries of Lector and Acolyte

The first section of canon 230 incorporates changes made by Pope Paul VI when he suppressed the minor orders and subdeaconate. In their stead (which were statuses reserved to clerics) he instituted the "lay ministry of acolyte" and the "lay ministry of lector." These are stable institutes for men only (but see below). They are also required for those seeking ordination as a deacon. It was a compromise measure. There was no inherent necessity to limit it to men and exclude women and there was no necessity to require them for ordination. Both of these are strong echoes of the previous clerical status of minor orders. The new code could have dropped both of these provisions, but it did not. In this country, they have generally fallen into disuse except for those seeking ordination. The new spirit of ministry for the laity still carries some of the burdensome restrictions of tradition.

Section two of this canon allows "lay persons" (as opposed to "lay men") to fulfill the function of lector "by temporary designation." Note that the ministry of acolyte is not mentioned in this section.

Section three is a pragmatic permission:

> [W]hen the need of the church warrants it and ministers are lacking, lay persons, even if they are not lectors or acolytes, can also supply certain of their duties, namely, to exercise the ministry of the word, to preside over liturgical prayers, to confer baptism, and to distribute Holy Communion, according to the prescripts of the law.

This exception to the rule has become the norm in many places. There have been strong tendencies to expand this as well as restrict this practice. A robust and healthy theology of baptism would push for further developments in this area. The shortage of ordained ministers pragmatically drives this trend forward.

Lay Ecclesiastical Employees

The first section of canon 231 states that people who are employed by the church ("devote themselves to special service of the church") are required to receive the necessary education and formation for their particular ministry or function. They are also obliged to fulfill their tasks "conscientiously, eagerly, and diligently."

The second section deals with remuneration and benefits. Excluding installed acolytes and lectors (see canon 230, §1), and after observing the legal requirements of the state, "lay persons have the right to decent remuneration appropriate to their conditions that they are able to provide decently for their own needs and those of their family. They also have a right for their social provision, social security, and health benefits to be duly provided." This is a remarkable list of rights. In this country there is a distinction between the "minimum wage" and a "living wage." It seems that the church argues for a living wage not just for an individual but for the whole family. Health insurance and retirement benefits are not optional, but are "to be duly provided." This obviously has serious ramifications for every bishop, pastor, and their respective finance councils.

These two lists of obligations and rights for all baptized persons in general and for all the laity in particular are seminal statements. Each needs to be developed through the customary practice of the church's administrators and through the jurisprudence of the ecclesiastical court system. What to do in the face of conflicts, personal limitations, personal sinfulness, and clashes of personality all have to be addressed and resolved in a Christian fashion. The biggest single danger to these obligations and rights is that they might be ignored.

Violated Rights

What can you do when someone violates on your rights? In the church there are two ways: administratively or judicially. One can either appeal to the superior or one can go to court. The church has both.

The preferred method is to make known whatever wrong has been done (at least in your opinion) to the person who made the wrong and then to his or her superior. Appeals can be made to the pastor, then to the bishop, and finally to the Vatican (generally through the Apostolic Nuncio in Washington, DC). Such appeals need to be well prepared and founded in law and not just in personal taste or whim. Few priests want their parish problems brought to the bishop. Fewer bishops want someone in the Vatican scrutinizing their decisions or policies. So there is generally a strong motivation to settle locally. If there is truly a violation of rights, merely walking away from it won't help. It should be addressed, but this entails a lot of work and stress.

The other method is to go to the Diocesan Tribunal (as long as the dispute is with someone under the bishop and not including the bishop). Anyone can ask that an advocate be appointed in order to help prepare and present the case. This is a much more difficult and technical approach than simply appealing to the superior.

The misuse of power must be addressed, otherwise dysfunctional systems develop. Knowing and vindicating rights is a powerful way to check the arbitrary use of power, and it empowers all the members of the church. Offices of Arbitration and Mediation exist for this purpose.

For Reflection and Discussion

1. What does equality mean to you?

2. How obedient do we have to be? What limits might there be to our obedience?

3. How do we divide resources between the school and the catechism program?

4. Are lectors and Eucharistic ministers mini-priests?

5. If you are unjustly treated, what should you do?

CHAPTER 8

Parish Governance

General Issues

Many issues can either build a community or tear it apart. Theology, liturgical style, music, and homilies can either inspire us or appall us. Money can as well. One reason why money is so powerful in relationships (marriage as well as parochial) is that it is measurable. There are no platitudes in bank statements, profit-and-loss reports, and balance sheets. The money is there or it is not. Issues may not be black and white, but finances are either "in the black" or "in the red." Given honesty—no fraud, tricks, or deceit—how money is handled is a clear and measurable way to establish exactly what a parish's priorities are. Much of canon law concerning money and management has to do with preventing fraud and balancing priorities.

Priorities, like job descriptions, pose an impossible dilemma in canon law. Generally everything is a priority. Lists of priorities in order of importance are not given. Nowhere does it say that social justice is more important than property insurance or a choir director is more important than a janitor. Anyone who has a cause can easily say, "This is a priority. It's in the Bible or in canon law!" That is not very helpful because almost everything is either in the Bible or canon law. When someone says "This is a priority" but does not say what it is prior to, in effect says nothing. The statement is useless. When everything is a priority, then everything is equal and therefore not a priority. Only when the person says that this particular issue or project is more important than "X" but less important than "Y" a meaningful statement is made.

Values clash when making or adjusting budgets. Canon law defines who is the decision maker, who is in a legal position to influence the decision maker, who can veto or stop the decision from being made, and what consequences could arise for breaking the law.

Parish Council and Finance Council

Juridic persons are corporations in the church. All parishes are "juridic persons" in the church (canon 515, §3). Each diocese and the Holy See are juridic persons. Many other institutions or groups of people can be either a public or a private juridic person in the church. By the very fact of being a juridic person in the church, it enjoys rights and obligations in the law.

But the pastor is the sole representative of the parish in all things legal and financial (canon 532). In American legal terminology, the pastor is like the trustee of a trust. He does not own it, but he makes decisions for it and for its benefit (not his own).

Therefore, the bishop cannot simply take money or land or buildings from the parish because he needs it or wants it. It does not belong to him, but to the parish. The pastor may find it in his personal best interests to comply with the bishop's wishes, but he must go through the finance council if the amount triggers laws compelling its advice or consent. He may also have to go through the parish council depending on its charter and bylaws. If the pastor and/or the finance council say no when its consent is needed, then the bishop must accept the decision.

Like every juridic person in the church, each parish must have a finance council (canons 1280, 536, §1) and obey the laws concerning the administration of goods (Book V of the Code of Canon Law, dealt with in Chapter 9). This finance council, while mandatory, has only one real power that is readily understood by Americans, the power of veto. But is also provides two others functions as well.

The first function is that of giving consent or veto. There are several types of transactions that a pastor, even though he is the sole person who can act in the name of the parish, must have the approval or consent of the finance council before he can act validly. If he does not get the approval, he cannot act.

The second function is that of giving the required advice or counsel. The finance council in all other respects is advisory. This second class of transactions requires that the pastor must listen to the finance council before he makes his decision and acts. The power to advise is not quite as appreciated by Americans as it is in the code. He does not have to agree with the finance council, but he must hear what they have to say. He would do well to follow their advice, but he is not bound to.

Unlike the U.S. Constitution which gives the Senate the power of advise and consent for international treaties and certain appointments, canon law separates the two for different classes of transactions. Generally, advice is required for the smaller decisions, while consent is required for larger ones. Of course, there is a whole arena of decisions and transactions that the pastor may decide at his own discretion requiring neither advice nor consent.

Advice and consent are both governed by canon 127. Everyone who is a member must be notified of the time and place of the meeting. If one-third of the members are not notified and do not show, then the meeting is invalid. When consent is required, an absolute majority of those present must give consent. When advice or counsel is required, everyone present is to be asked to give advice (canon 127, §1). When consent is required, the pastor who does not get it acts invalidly (canon 127, §2, 1°). When advice or counsel is required, the pastor also acts invalidly if he does not get it. He does not have to follow it, but, he must hear it for validity. The canon further advises the pastor: "[A]lthough not obliged to accept their opinion even if unanimous, a superior is nonetheless not to act contrary to that opinion, especially if unanimous, without a reason which is overriding in the superior's judgment"(canon 127, §2, 2°). The moral judgment of the council enjoys the presumption of the law, even if it can be overruled.

The third function is the free give-and-take of ideas regarding the parish. This resembles a "think tank." Budget development and new fund-raising programs generally surface during these types of sessions.

In no case is the finance council a legislature. Only the bishop has legislative power and he cannot even delegate it. The finance council cannot take initiatives by telling the pastor he must do this or that. The pastor presides over the meeting (there should not be a separate president or chairman) and the pastor sets the agenda. Technically, the finance council responds to the pastor's initiative. The council must be heard on some occasions, and, less frequently, it has a veto that can stop the pastor from doing something. The biggest activity of the finance council is being a think tank for the free flow of ideas.

The parish council is required only "if the diocesan bishop judges it opportune after he has heard the presbyteral council" (canon 536, §1). The pastor presides. When the parish council has an independent president or chairperson with other officers, it gives the American public the idea that it is like the legislature, separate but equal with the pastor. Not true. This is an advisory group that has no power to "make the pastor do something," nor does it have the power of veto, as the finance council has. It possesses only a consultative vote. Nor does the pastor have to bring issues to it "to be heard," as the bishop must do with the presbyteral council for establishing parish councils themselves in the first place, nor as pastors must do with the finance council for certain transactions. It is a think tank for the pastor with moral persuasion for both the pastor himself and the parish at large. It is to be a center of organizational expertise and motivation to assist the pastor and be a vehicle of communication between the parish and its pastor. The bishop may give the parish council a stronger consultative role in the by-laws and decrees established in the diocese, but the bishop cannot give it a power or role that according to the code properly belongs to the pastor.

For Reflection and Discussion

1. What is the distinction between legal decision making power and legal influence?
2. How influential is influence?
3. What precisely is the function of the finance council?
4. What precisely is the function of the parish council?

CHAPTER 9

Parish Finances and Property

Book V of the Code of Canon Law concerns the temporal goods of the church. Everything in this book is quite abstract and general. The word "temporal" is distinguished from "spiritual" goods. Spiritual goods are sacraments, preaching, and so on. Temporal goods are buildings, art, money, and the like.

The word "parish" is not even mentioned. Instead, it should be known that "a legitimately erected parish possesses juridic personality by the law itself" (canon 515, §3), and that since "a parish is a certain community of the Christian faithful stably constituted in a particular church" (a diocese) (canon 515, §1), then it must be an "aggregate of persons" which is "non-collegial," that is, everyone is *not* equal (canon 115).

Since this is all established by the law itself, then a parish is a *public juridic person*; this phrase appears in Book V frequently. Parishes are not the only example of public juridic persons, but they are the majority. The diocese itself is a distinct public juridic person. Each parish is a distinct public juridic person distinct from the diocese and distinct from every other parish or any other juridic person. Other public juridic persons include formal houses of pontifically recognized religious orders and congregations. This might include monasteries, friaries, schools, hospitals, and other apostolates owned by them. Public juridic persons are to be distinguished from *private* juridic persons and from physical persons (an actual individual human being). Private juridic persons are established by the bishop and have less canonical oversight (that is, they are more independent) than the public juridic persons.

So for our purposes here, whenever we read the terms "juridic person" in general, or "public juridic person," in particular, it refers to the parish (along with all the other entities in its class). Many people don't make the connection between a parish and a juridic person and so miss the application to the parish. Also, the word "church" means any *public* juridic person (canon 1258), which includes the Holy See, the diocese, the parish, the monastery, the pontifical right religious order, and so on.

So, what does the church need money for? Temporal goods (as opposed to spiritual goods) includes money and all that money can buy. Canon 1254, §2 lists the principal proper purposes of temporal goods:

> to order divine worship,
> to care for the decent support of the clergy and other ministers,
> and to exercise works of the sacred apostolate
> and of charity, especially toward the needy.

These four purposes, or goals, include everything from building a cathedral and buying vestments and books to paying teachers' social security in the Catholic school and subsidizing soups kitchens or sending money to foreign missions.

Therefore, fundamental to every juridic person (both public and private) is the fact that it is "capable of acquiring, retaining, administering, and alienating temporal goods according to the norm of law" (canon 1255). So "ownership of goods belongs to that juridic person which has acquired them legitimately" (canon 1256). All these things owned by *public* juridic persons are now ecclesiastical goods and are governed by canon law and the statutes of the juridic person (canon 1257).

This means that parish goods (including money) belong to the parish and not the pastor or the bishop or the pope. The pope does not own the church, but all ownership is subject to his authority (canon 1256). The pope does not own the dioceses of the world, nor does the bishop own his own diocese, even though he may be a "corporation sole" in some states. (This is a legal form of incorporation where authority is vested in one person. In the case of a diocese, that person is the diocesan bishop.) The bishop does not own the parishes, even if all of them are in his name. The pastor does not own the parish, neither its property nor its money.

The public juridic person owns it (whether the universal church, the diocesan or particular church, or the parish church).

But these churches are not democracies either. Each is a *non-collegial* juridic person. This means that not everyone in the parish or the diocese can get together and vote on everything with an equal voice. Someone must be the decision maker. For the parish church, it is the pastor (canon 532). For the diocesan or particular church, it is the bishop (canon 381, §1). For the universal church, it is the Roman Pontiff (canon 332, §1). Each is like the sole trustee for the trust.

Not surprisingly, the bishop can "moderately tax" all parishes and other public juridic persons in his diocese for the sake of diocesan needs (canon 1263). What is surprising is that this is a new provision in the 1983 code. Theoretically the diocese was to have a sufficient benefice (source of money), so that it did not need to, or could, tax parishes, which likewise were supposedly endowed by a benefice. Each had their own property and sometimes a parish could be wealthier than the diocese, or a diocese wealthier than the Vatican. But in the U.S. benefices never really existed as they did in Europe, so taxation was customary, even though it was contrary to the then current canon law. There was no other source of money. Now the bishop can tax "moderately." This tax is also to be proportional.

Bishops also authorize special collections for specific parish, diocesan, national, or global projects. They also set the limits on how much can be set for offerings for sacraments and sacramentals (canon 1264, §2). This can be a problem. There can be cultural clashes on giving money to the church. Some cultures have the expectation that one should give to the church regularly—every Sunday. They expect small offerings for Mass intentions, baptisms, weddings, and such. Other cultures have the custom of "paying as you go" or for "services rendered." They do not give regularly but only when some occasion calls for it (baptisms, weddings, funerals, special blessings). They can be very generous in these instances and give much more than the regulations allow. It is a balancing of "what to ask for" and "what can you accept."

There is a remarkable, precise presumption set into the law regarding voluntary offerings: "Unless the contrary is established, offerings given to superiors or administrators of any ecclesiastical juridic person, even a private one, are presumed given to the juridic person itself" (canon 1267, §1). This means that if someone *silently* hands the pastor a $100 bill after a wedding or funeral, then the presumption is that this particular $100 goes into the parish account and not his personal account. Sometimes the pastor may cough and clear his throat and ask if it is for the church or for him. If the donor says, "It's for you, Father. Go have a good meal," then he can keep it. Otherwise not.

Similarly, gifts cannot be refused except for a just cause. In matters of greater importance, a pastor needs the bishop's permission to refuse a gift. This occasion may arise in the case of illegally obtained money (drugs, organized crime, extortion, prostitution, pornography, etc.). Sometimes an unsavory individual who happens to be wealthy might also want social respectability, too. One way of attaining that might be through a "significant donation" to the church. If the gift is to be refused, the bishop's permission is required (canon 1267, §2).

On the other hand, if the gift contains significant conditions attached to it, then the bishop's permission is required to accept it. If the conditions actually worsen the overall financial welfare (patrimony) of the parish, then all the canons on alienation apply. (Patrimony is the composite of all the factors making up the financial welfare of the parish. Alienation is the worsening of the patrimony. Both of these terms refer to the long-range welfare of the parish.)

Let's look at this situation: A parish needs $100,000 because the parish bookkeeper forgot to pay taxes on the employees for five years. The parish needs the money now or the pastor or bishop will go to jail. A donor comes by and offers to give the parish the money on the condition that it has a Mass said for him annually on his birthday forever. The bishop needs to approve the donation because the obligation continues even after the parish no longer exists and even after the diocese is suppressed. The obligation always goes to the next higher authority in the hierarchy. "Forever" is a long time. When it comes to future obligations, the bishop needs to approve establishing an obligation "forever."

A second alternative is that the donor will give the parish the $100,000 on the condition that when he retires, the parish will give him one million dollars. He wants a safety net in old age and figures the church will last until he retires and dies. The bishop must approve this donation. The bishop also must immediately follow all the procedures required for alienation because of the amount of money to be paid out when the donor retires will certainly eventually harm the parish's patrimony. This immediately becomes a liability for that parish.

A third basic principle given in this canon is that "offerings given by the faithful for a certain purpose can be applied only for that same purpose" (canon 1267, §3). *No one can divert the funds to another purpose without the donor's permission.* That "no one" includes the pastor and the bishop. There are complications when the donor is dead or otherwise unavailable, but this basic principle is always the starting point.

Another general principle in this introductory section to Book V is that sacred objects (chalices, vestments, monstrances, altars) that belong to the parish cannot be given or sold to anyone (that is, a physical person), nor to a private juridic person, but only to another public juridic person (such as another parish, a religious order, a diocese). One cannot clean out the sacristy and auction its contents as a way to raise funds.

Administration of Goods

The second canon of this title deals with "social provision" for the clergy (canon 1274, §1, 2) and "to satisfy obligations toward other persons who serve the church and meet the various needs of the diocese" (canon 1274, §3). These are vague and broad terms that are not easily enforceable in a contentious litigation, but they do set a tone for social justice that the diocese has toward the clergy and those employed by the church.

A far-reaching principle for parishes is established in canon 1276. The bishop is to exercise "careful vigilance" over the administration of all the goods that belong to any public juridic person subject to him. A pontifically-recognized religious order would not be subject to the bishop here. The bishop likewise is to "take care of the ordering of the entire matter of the administration of ecclesiastical goods by issuing special instructions within the limits of universal and particular law." This means that he has the duty to oversee all finances, property, bookkeeping, audits, and investments. This is extremely broad. Likewise he is to issue regulations on how to administer ecclesiastical goods, which includes everything that the parish owns. He is limited in that he must obey universal law, that is, laws from the Vatican for the whole church, and particular laws, that is, laws issued by the Vatican for the United States in particular, decrees from the United States Conference of Catholic Bishops, which bind all dioceses of the country, decrees of an ecclesiastical province binding the metropolitan see (archdiocese) and all its suffragan sees (dioceses), laws promulgated by the bishop for his own diocese.

The bishop cannot, therefore, claim parish property, money, or investments for diocesan use. Why? The diocese is one juridic person and the parish is another juridic person. Each of them has the right to own its own property. No one can just take from another. He can "moderately tax" but not "immoderately" so. Convincing the bishop of that distinction might be a difficult matter, which is why both the finance council and the presbyteral council must be heard.

The bishop can, though, *legislate* (using legislative power which he alone has for making particular law for his diocese) and *regulate* (using executive power, which the vicar general also has) for the issuing of instructions and regulations on:

- how the parish maintains its books
- procedures it must use for the collection and safekeeping of cash
- how it is to bank its money
- what it is to do with surplus money (for example, where and how it is saved or invested)
- how, when, and what financial reports are to be filed with the diocese
- when the parish will endure a financial audit or an operational or procedural audit, and who will do it.

Both the bishop and the vicar general, using executive power, can dispense from any and all of these laws, except those regarding the nature and rights of a juridic person.

As mentioned above, every juridic person is to have its own finance council or at least two counselors who are to assist the administrator in fulfilling his function (canon 1280). This means the parish must have a finance council who helps the pastor. This help is so important that the pastor invalidly acts when he exceeds the limits and manner of ordinary administration, unless he has first obtained a written faculty from the bishop (canon 1281, §1). The bishop determines for the parishes of his diocese exactly what is "the limit and manner of ordinary administration" after having heard his own diocesan financial council (canon 1281, §2).

Curiously, there is a double standard in the next section of this canon that distinctly favors the institution: *"Unless and to the extent that it is to its own advantage,* a juridic person (a parish or diocese or religious order) is *not* bound to answer for acts invalidly placed by its administrators." So if the pastor has the chance to buy the Louisiana Purchase cheap, but it is beyond the parish's limits and he does it anyway, then, *if* it is to the parish's advantage, it can be all right. But if it is not to the parish's advantage, the parish can renounce the action as invalid.

Canon law also makes a distinction that we do not have in American law: "invalidity" versus "illicitly." In the United States, something is either legal or illegal. If it is illegal then it is punishable and can be thrown out as not binding. For the church, "illicit" means that it is against the law and is punishable, but it is still valid and cannot be thrown out. Fundamentally it still exists and it is still effective. The one who did it can be punished for breaking the law. "Invalid" is deeper and more radical in its effects. It is not only illicit, but it is also not effective and does not exist. This is rare and reserved for "the *most* important things," as opposed to merely "important things."

This distinction is crucial in the effects of canon 1281, §3. If the pastor or bishop or any other administrator of a juridic person in the church goes beyond his competency and does something invalid, then that parish or diocese is not bound to answer for it. If it is advantageous and the parish wants it, then it can accept it. If it is disadvantageous, then the parish can choose either to accept it anyway or to ignore it.

However, if the pastor or bishop does something less offensive to the law and "only" does something illicitly, then the parish or diocese is bound by the action. But the parish or diocese can have recourse against the pastor or bishop because he broke the law and thus is liable to punishment.

The rest of this section deals with principles of administration that can seem obvious at first but are listed here because of a history of problems with each of them. Applying these generalities to the pastor in particular, he is:

- Bound to administer all the ecclesiastical goods of a parish in the name of the church according to the norm of law (canon 1282). He is not to administer them in his own name.

- To take an oath before the bishop that when he takes office he will administer well and faithfully; that he is "to prepare and sign an accurate and clear inventory of immovable property, movable objects, whether precious or of some cultural value, or other goods, with their description and appraisal; any inventory already done is to be reviewed"; and to put a copy of the inventory in the diocesan files and keep it current regarding the parish's patrimony (canon 1283). This is to help solve the problem of knowing, when a priest dies or is transferred, what belonged to him and what belonged to the parish.

- "To fulfill his function with the diligence of a good householder" (canon 1284, §1). This and several of the following items are listed specifically because there is not a particular canon on negligence. These canons try to cover what American law would call "lack of due diligence" or "negligence."

- To see that nothing is lost or damaged and that the parish is insured (canon 1284, §2, 1°).

- To make sure that ownership is protected both in canon law and in American law (canon 1284, §2). This is a particularly difficult goal. Each state has its own laws on ownership of property. In American law, bishops sometimes own the property of the diocese and of all the parishes. Sometimes they are the head of a corporation that owns it all. Canon law does not recognize that. The problem painfully arises when the bishop and the diocese are being sued.

- To observe civil and canon law, observe restrictions and wishes of a founder or a donor and be "especially on guard so that no damage comes to the church from the non-observance of civil laws" (canon 1282, §2, 3°). The intention of the donor is again stressed here. It is mentioned and protected many times throughout the Code. Also the canon does not exempt the church from American law, but rather obligates the pastor and bishop to comply with American law.

- To "collect the return of goods and the income accurately and on time, protect what is collected, and use them according to the intention of the founder or legitimate norms" (canon 1284, §2, 4°). Procedures for counting and banking the Sunday collections can be a problem addressed by the bishop under this rubric.
- To "pay at the stated time the interest due on a loan or mortgage and take care that the capital debt itself is repaid in a timely manner" (canon 1284, §2, 5°).
- "With the consent of the ordinary, invest the money that is left over after expenses and can be usefully set aside for the purposes of the juridic person" (canon 1284, §2, 6°).
- To "keep well-organized books of receipts and expenditures" (canon 1284, §2, 7°).
- To "draw up a report of the administration at the end of each year" (canon 1284, §2, 8°).
- To "organize correctly and protect in a suitable and proper archive the documents and records on which the property rights of the church…are based and deposit authentic copies of them in the archive of the curia when it can be done conveniently" (canon 1284, §2, 9°).
- Strongly recommended to prepare a budget (canon 1284, §3).
- To make donations for piety or charity but within limits: only within the limits of "ordinary administration" and from "moveable goods" that do not belong to the patrimony of the parish (canon 1285).
- To observe meticulously the civil laws concerning labor and social policy (canon 1286, 1°).
- To pay a just and decent wage to employees so that they are able to provide fittingly for their own needs and those of their dependents (canon 1286, 2°).
- To present an annual report to the bishop "who is to present it for examination by the finance council; any contrary custom is reprobated" (canon 1287, §1). The final clause of this section of the canon is a

very strong statement that one cannot claim contrary custom and refuse to present an annual report to the bishop.

- To "render an account to the faithful concerning the goods offered by the faithful to the church" (canon 1287, §2). This gives the people a right to know how the money they donate to the parish is spent.

- To "Neither initiate nor contest litigation in a civil forum in the name of the public juridic person unless they have obtained the written permission of their own ordinary" (canon 1288). A civil judge probably would not accept a pastor as the respondent in a case refusing to show up in court because he does not have the bishop's permission.

- "Administrators cannot relinquish their function on their own initiative; if the church is harmed from an arbitrary withdrawal, moreover, they are bound to restitution" (canon 1289). Most resignations must be accepted to become effective. One just cannot walk away without consequences.

These specific items are alluded to in the general responsibilities of a pastor, an "impossible job description."

Financial Categories in Canon Law

The first title of Book V on "The Temporal Goods of the Church" deals with the acquisition of money. Income is generally not that controversial. Anyone can put money into your account. The second title deals with administration, taking care of what you have and reporting to those who belong to your parish and to the bishop. The third title, though, is more delicate: spending. What are the limits of what anyone can do regarding spending the parish's assets. Not everyone can sign a check. Some checks need more scrutiny than others.

Because canon law deals with the whole Latin Rite of the universal church, it must legislate in sufficiently abstract terms that are applicable to us in the United States as well as to the various other economies of the world. These terms will be applied to the United States only. Each country will have different applications of each concept. In fact, each diocese of the United States can and does have its own application of these principles for its parishes. The Archdioceses of Boston and New York have a radically distinct culture, financial base, and custom than does the Diocese of Gallup in New Mexico and Arizona, which is primarily composed of the Navajo Nation and the Hopi Indians. Applications within a particular diocese must be made by the bishop sensitive to the particular church he leads.

These terms are:

- Acts of Ordinary Administration
- Acts of Extraordinary Administration
- Acts of Administration "which are more important in light of the economic condition of the diocese"
- Maximum limit
- Minimum limit
- Patrimony
- Alienation.

As noted, these terms are vague and obtuse because of the global reach of the code for all Latin Rite Catholics scattered around the world. But the Code does define who is competent to apply these terms to the churches on the national and the diocesan level and to the individual juridic person.

Any individual parish is subject to all these different levels of legislation and regulation: the Roman Pontiff and the Code of Canon Law, the regulations of the various departments in the Vatican, the binding norms of the United States Conference of Catholic Bishops, the local legislation and regulations published by the ecclesiastical province (the archbishop and his fellow bishops in an particular area), the legislation and regulations published by an individual bishop for his diocese, the statutes of the individual parish, and finally the directions of the pastor. Like Russian nesting dolls where each fits inside another, so all these levels of legislation and regulation must fit within each other. The Roman Pontiff is the most powerful legislator, but the personality and the knowledge of the pastor is the most immediate.

Acts of Ordinary Administration

These involve the daily running of the parish: collecting money, paying bills, maintaining and repairing buildings, hiring and firing employees, following the budget. As a general rule, if it is in the budget, it is ordinary.

The pastor does not need any special consultation or permission to do these things once the budget is approved.

Acts of Extraordinary Administration

As mentioned above in canon 1281, §1, the pastor acts invalidly without the bishop's prior permission. Because every parish is a juridic person, every parish is supposed to have specific statutes at the time of its establishment (canons 94, 117). As a practical matter, most parishes do not have specific statutes and therefore would fall under the regulatory authority of the bishop, after hearing the financial council (canon 1281, §2). If the parish is a civil corporation, then its by-laws would also apply. If the parish has both civil by-laws and ecclesiastical statutes, then it must abide by both. Also, each diocese would have its own set of guidelines defining what is "ordinary administration" versus "extraordinary administration." In general "acts of extraordinary administration are those which because of the nature or importance of the act itself, or its financial value, require the permission of a higher authority. Examples of extraordinary acts include those acts which do not occur on a regular basis, such as purchase of land, construction of new buildings or extensive repair or remodeling of buildings, expenditures over a designated financial amount, refusal of major bequests, purchase or replacement of major equipment, and the dedication of surplus funds."[1]

Acts of Administration Related to the Economy

This category refers only to the diocese. It is different than extraordinary administration which is established for dioceses by the United States Conference of Catholic Bishops. The bishop and his consultors and advisors should determine when these consultations must be made for the "more important" category.

Patrimony

In general this would be the long-term fixed and liquid assets of the parish (or any other juridic person). These are the things that are there perma-

---

1. Kevin McKenna, Lawrence DiNardo, and Joseph Pokusa, eds., *Church Finance Handbook* (Washington, DC, Canon Law Society of America, 1999), p. 193.

nently for the future good of the parish: land, buildings, long-term funds of various kinds of investments. These are the things that must be preserved for the future as well as helping in the present. It is the "inheritance" of the parish from the past as well as what it bequeaths to its future. No one administrator (pastor) has total control over its use. Since the new Code (1983), if some significantly large donation is made to the parish, it can be designated as "stable patrimony," thus placing it under the restrictions needed for "alienation" and thus beyond the scope of the current pastor to use it all at his discretion. If this is not done, then the pastor is not bound to the laws of alienation, although he is still bound to the spending limits of ordinary versus extraordinary administration. "It has been the consistent praxis of canon law that those assets that are necessary to a public juridic person in order to accomplish the ends for which it was established are a part of stable patrimony of that juridic person and may not be freely alienated."[2]

Alienation

Alienation is a very broad concept that basically refers to the lessening or the loss of any or all interest of or any potential risk to the stable patrimony of the parish or diocese. Complete interest is the complete ownership of the property (any property, not just land). Partial interest refers to leases, mortgages, options on, use of, easements, liens, control or authority over. A parish can lose complete interest in property by selling it outright or giving it away. A parish can lose partial interest in a property by selling, leasing, or mortgaging some aspect of the property, even though retaining ownership. These are covered by canon 1291. But some significant transactions that do not directly affect the patrimony of the parish could still put that patrimony at risk by depleting other resources that the parish has. This, too, is covered by alienation and is mandated by canon 1295. So there are two "fences" protecting the stable assets of the parish: alienation of canon 1291 (protecting the patrimony itself) and of canon 1295 (protecting the buffer zone around the patrimony).

---

2. McKenna, 193.

Maximum Limit

This is the limit no one can approve within the juridic person. Recourse to a higher authority is needed. No one, it seems, likes to have limits placed on his authority to act. Pastors don't like it and neither do bishops. The maximum limit for a diocese is the limit beyond which a bishop must seek authorization from the Vatican to act. The United States Conference of Catholic Bishops is to propose the maximum and minimum limits to the Congregation for Bishops for final approval. For many years they didn't propose anything. The congregation then on its own imposed limits. The conference countered with a higher set of limits (double what the Congregation of Bishops decreed). On January 1, 2004, new norms became effective for the Latin Dioceses in the United States: But that was only half of what the bishops requested. They appealed, and on March 31, 2004, the Congregation for Bishops "by way of exception" granted a two-year exemption so that the maximum until 2006 was ten million dollars for larger dioceses and five million dollars for smaller.

These are the maximum limits for any transaction a bishop may do within his diocese without authorization from the Vatican. But in order to do these transactions, he must first fulfill the requirements of the minimum limit.

Minimum Limit

This is the threshold where neither the bishop nor the pastor can approve the transaction and must receive consent from within the juridic person (the diocese or the parish). This minimum limit sets the norm for when the bishop cannot decide alone but must obtain the consent of his College of Consultors, the Diocesan Finance Council, and "those concerned" (e.g., the donors who retained some right or set a condition on their donation, if this applies to the particular transaction). "Obtaining consent" means that any one of these three groups can veto the transaction.

The parish, too, has limits established by the Vatican for the United States. The Congregation for Bishops has decreed that parishes (actually any juridic person under the bishop) cannot exceed a maximum of five million dollars without going to the bishop for approval. They also decreed that the pastor may not decide by himself any transactions larger than $25,000 or, if higher, five percent of ordinary income. As noted in the previous section the pastor must get consent of the parish finance council. But these are the Vatican limits.[3]

The bishop also may have regulations governing parishes more restrictive than this. The bishop's regulations may not be more liberal than these limits. If the parish or other juridic person under the bishop has statutes, then the statutes or bylaws may be more restrictive but not more liberal than the Vatican limits.

So, under the exception granted by the Congregation for Bishops, a pastor may have discretionary decision making regarding expenditures or alienation up to $12,500 (or the five percent amount of last year's budget if higher than $12,500). Once the pastor reaches that minimum amount he must get the consent of his finance council. If the requested alienation reaches the amount of five million, then the pastor, after getting the consent of his finance council, must get consent from the bishop.

To further confuse this, every year these amounts change according to the CPI (the Consumer Price Index or the inflation figure) from the previous year.

The Vatican has extended its exception for this until 2008. All of these issues can be addressed at the Web site of the United States Conference of Catholic Bishops in Washington, DC (www.usccb.org) on its Canonical Affairs Department page.

Obviously this is very confusing. Without a clear understanding of what these terms and levels of authority mean, it is impossible to understand what is allowed, forbidden, or discretionary. Because the various administrators and their critics often don't understand this material, the person with the highest title or most-intimidating style frequently prevails— whether or not he or she is correct.

On the most practical level, parishes should consult with the Diocesan Financial Officer to know what should be done in a specific case.

---

3. These Vatican limits are also "by way of exception" until 2008. Then they fall to $2,500,000 for the maximum without the bishop's consent and $12,500 or, if higher, five percent of the ordinary income noted in the previous year's budget for the minimum level.

For Reflection and Discussion

1. How is your parish structured according to state law?
2. Is this compatible with canon law structures?
3. If the bishop files for bankruptcy, do parishes fall under the Bankruptcy Court's jurisdiction?
4. Do parishes have to sell assets to pay for fines and penalties of other parishes?

CHAPTER 10

Tensions between Canon Law and American Law from a Canonical Perspective

As Americans, we take for granted a written constitution, a bill of rights, the separation of powers, the separation of church and state. Unless we are quite familiar with our own history, we may not realize how our bold ancestors in the 1770s and later struggled mightily toward the evolution of our "great experiment." Even fourscore and seven years later, Abraham Lincoln voiced their concerns which were also his: whether a nation governed by the people and for the people will perish from the earth. Looking back, it seems clear and quite evident. At the time, it did not.

The church does not have a written constitution, a bill of rights, a separation of powers, or the separation of church and state. Recently several attempts were made to come up with a written constitution but they failed. We have the Scriptures and we have tradition, but we do not have a "fundamental law" which is the basis of our laws and structures. Such a "fundamental law" could not be changed by a pope or ecumenical council. Our rock-solid foundation is based on Scripture.

The church did not have a code of canon law until 1917. Prior to that, there was a "corpus of canon law," a body of law. It was the accumulation of centuries of decisions and decrees of popes and councils plus a megadose of custom. Actually it was not unlike English common law over the centuries—except that the church's body of tradition started around 48–49 AD with the Council of Jerusalem fighting over the requirements of the Mosaic Law for Gentile followers of the Risen Lord. Justinian had a code and Napoleon had a code. After the Napoleonic experience, codes of laws came into favor. The church decided to have one of its own and in 1917 promulgated the first Code. In 1983, Pope John Paul II promulgated the second Code of the church. The first Code did not have a list of rights; the second Code did.

The concept of the separation of powers (that is, executive, legislative, and judicial) was strongly argued during the Enlightenment before the French Revolution. Prior to that, all three powers were radically vested in the sovereign, whether king, pope, or another kind of ruler. The pope is still the supreme executive, the supreme legislator, and the supreme judge. All three of these powers separate under him, but they are all vested in him on the universal level. The bishop is the same on the diocesan level. The source of all executive, legislative, and judicial power in a diocese flows from the bishop. The law delegates his executive power to the vicar general of the diocese and his judicial power to the judicial vicar of the diocese. The bishop cannot delegate his legislative power to anyone. He is the sole legislator in the diocese.

Balance of power, then, is approximated not with competing governmental functions, as in the United States, but in broadening the exercise of that power by councils that have a veto or a mandatory consultative voice. Moral persuasion is employed rather than constitutional rivalry.

The idea of the separation of the church and the state was unthinkable to most people, even during the Enlightenment. Religion was seen as the glue of society and culture, keeping people together. The Founding Fathers knew very well that this was a new and dangerous concept. It looked difficult enough to them back then when almost everyone who counted was white, Anglo-Saxon, and Protestant. Catholic immigration challenged the mix, as did Jewish immigration. The influx of atheism with its constitutional protections and then Islam and the religion/philosophies of Asia have stretched the two religion clauses of the First Amendment further than many people are willing to allow. The broad social accommodation of Protestant Christianity into many governmental activities (chaplains,

Christmas scenes in front of the courthouse, prayer in school) was challenged, sometimes successfully.

Fundamentalism is largely seen as a reaction to a secular society with its non-judgmental tolerance and acceptance of the many variations of lifestyle, and to the Supreme Court's rejection of Christian symbols and activities in governmental activities. Fundamentalism can be seen as a failure of that great experiment in separating the church from the state. The church is now seen legally as merely a "volunteer society" with no special legal standing to influence government and society. Yet it has a First Amendment guarantee to free exercise and a prohibition from being established by the federal government and later by state government.

PART III

American Civil Law and the Parish

David McNeill, Jr.

Introduction

Before you read anything else in this section, you must understand that it will not make you a lawyer. It will not give you the tools to handle legal actions or perform your own legal services. The fact of the matter is that nothing, absolutely nothing, will substitute for good legal advice based upon a complete presentation of all facts to a competent attorney. If you learn nothing else from Part III, remember that good legal advice, preferably in advance of a problem, is the best—and ultimately, least expensive—legal protection you can get for your parish or yourself.

Why should you read this, then? There are three reasons. First, by having a basic understanding of the principles discussed here, you will be better able to spot potential legal problems and avoid them. Second, if you should need to contact an attorney, you will have a better idea of the questions he or she may ask and the information you will need to provide. Third, by understanding the basic principles outlined here, you should have a better understanding of what is going on in your case.

We hope you can avoid legal difficulties, or, if you do have any, you will have a better idea of what is happening. Our purpose here is to alert you to basic concepts and provide guidance in avoiding legal problems, a far better approach than paying to solve them after they arise. The main theme of this section is that you should strive to avoid legal difficulties, not litigate them.[1]

The legal discussions that follow will cover civil law issues only. It will not (except where we point out differences between criminal and civil law) discuss criminal issues. It is important to note, however, that the same act may give rise to both a civil action and a criminal action. This question is discussed in further detail in the chapter on legal concepts.

---

1. This is also consistent with canon 1288: "Administrators are neither to initiate nor to contest a lawsuit on behalf of a public juridic person in civil court unless they obtain the written permission of their own ordinary."

It is vitally important to understand that there are few, if any, absolutes in the law. If, however, there are any immutables, two are of vital importance here: every rule has at least one exception or variation, and the facts of each case determine which rules apply and how they are applied. Keep these principles in mind as you consider your situation and the points made in the following chapters.

Finally, we can't overstress that whenever a legal question arises, you should consult an attorney competent in the area of concern. These pages can only provide you with concepts, not legal advice. If you have a question whether any course of action you are considering is proper, you should consult an attorney to determine whether it is in keeping with your state's law as well as federal law. It is most unwise for non-lawyers to attempt to draft legally binding documents or resolve legal problems without professional help. It is far less expensive, and often faster, to have an attorney guide you through such matters from the beginning.

CHAPTER 11

Canon Law and Civil Law

A pastor I knew was not happy when his civil lawyer told him he couldn't hold another parish raffle. State law permitted only two raffles per year, and he wanted to hold a third. Exasperated at what he considered an arbitrary rule that was getting in the way of his parish's needs, the pastor pronounced, "Well, that's all fine and good, Mr. Attorney, but I am bound by canon law, not your civil law!"

The lawyer quietly responded with an important consideration: "Well, Father, when you tell that to the civil judge just before he imposes the sentence for violating the civil law, I'm sure he will understand completely." Thankfully, that wry comment got the pastor's attention and he decided to wait until the following year to hold his raffle. In fact, canons 1284 and 1286 impose an obligation to comply with civil law. The fact is, the church has no choice but to live within the civil law since it is the governing law for those who are not part of the church and also provides it essential protection. It is also a question of social obligation.

Even though many people seem to think that church and civil government are in a state of constant conflict, canon law and civil law are generally compatible, or, at least not at loggerheads with each other. Hollywood, for example, often makes much of how the seal of confession[1] creates a conflict between the priest who heard the murderer's confession and the detective's need for that precise information to put the evildoer in

---

1. Canon 983.

prison. In fact, such stories are just that. Every state in the union, and the federal laws, provide for confidentiality between the clergy and those who communicate with them in that capacity. Note the phraseology of the last sentence. Most laws protect all communications between clergy and anyone who communicates with them in that capacity.[2] Thus, under civil law, the privilege covers more than communications made in the confessional. It would include communications to deacons that were meant by the person to remain confidential, or in civil law parlance, privileged.

While it is true that canon law and civil law can conflict with one another, these conflicts rarely create head-to-head battles. For example, the ban on abortion found in canon law is not the civil law of the United States, yet no U.S. court has ever forced a Catholic hospital to perform an abortion, despite several lawsuits attempting to obtain such a result. In highly emotionally-charged situations, such as abortion rallies, it is easy to lose sight of this fact.

The relationship between civil and canon law is relatively simple. The civil law will view canon law as the church's internal regulations. That is, just as corporations such as General Motors have their own by-laws and other regulations governing their internal operations, the church has its canon law. Nevertheless, in the eyes of the civil law, an organization's internal regulations cannot supersede the civil law. That is why when a diocese, parish, or other Catholic group wants to incorporate (for exam-

---

2. For example, the New Mexico Rules of Evidence express the civil view of privileged communications to clergy in this way:

11–506. Communications to clergy.

A. Definitions. As used in this rule:

  (1) a "member of the clergy" is a minister, priest, rabbi or other similar functionary of a religious organization, or an individual reasonably believed so to be by the person consulting that person;

  (2) a communication is "confidential" if made privately and not intended for further disclosure except to other persons present in furtherance of the purpose of the communication.

B. General rule of privilege. A person has a privilege to refuse to disclose and to prevent another from disclosing a confidential communication by the person to a member of the clergy as a spiritual adviser.

C. Who may claim the privilege. The privilege may be claimed by the person or by the person's guardian, conservator or, upon death, personal representative. The member of the clergy may claim the privilege on behalf of the person. The authority to claim the privilege is presumed in the absense of evidence to the contrary.

ple, to obtain tax-free status), it must do so in accordance with the civil law of the state where it will incorporate. It is also why parishes are bound by limitations on the number of raffles allowed, federal and state sexual harassment laws, criminal law, and so on.

If we understand that both sets of rules are intended to govern our people for the good of all, we can understand that both sets of laws are beneficial and, as a general and practical matter, create schemes that benefit their particular societies. Where conflicts do occur, consultation with a civil or canon lawyer—or both—can often lead to a solution that violates neither set of norms. Above all, we have to remember that both sets of laws are for the common good; we must seek to comply with their letter and spirit to the greatest extent possible.

For Reflection and Discussion

1. Discuss some ways you see canon law and civil law interacting. For example, the debate over abortion, the clergy sex scandal, and laws on marriage and divorce.
2. Discuss the ways in which civil law is written. How does this differ from canon law?
3. Consider and discuss how the moral law (e.g., the Ten Commandments and other ethical codes) can and should impact the writing and interpretation of civil laws.

CHAPTER 12

General Civil Law Concepts

The American system of justice is based upon several basic concepts that apply to almost every legal issue. This chapter will provide an overview of some of those concepts as well as a general discussion of how the legal system is supposed to operate.

History

American law is derived from the law of England. The English law with which we are familiar began in 1066 when William the Conqueror defeated Britain in the Battle of Hastings. He brought with him a new legal system based upon a plan of national courts presided over by appointed judges who rode circuits to bring a common form of justice to all people. This replaced the previous system of tribal courts each with their own rules and ideals of justice.

As the citizens of European countries moved into the New World, they brought with them their own sets of laws: the Spaniards brought Spanish law to the Southwest and parts of the West Coast; the British brought their law to the East Coast; the French imported their law to Louisiana.

After the Revolutionary War, the United States expanded westward bringing with it the law that had been used in the original Thirteen Colonies, the law of England. The legal concepts and procedures of this legal system became the basic form of law for the United States. Remnants of the other legal forms were, however, kept by various states. Thus, eight of the United States still use the Spanish law concept of community property when dealing with how married couples hold property. Louisiana has kept the French concept of law in which one court decision is not necessarily precedent for a later, similar case.[1]

American law further carved its own niche by instituting the concept of federalism. Under this system the central national—federal—government legislates certain aspects of law for the entire country, while the independent states control the other aspects of their local populace. Thus, the states regulate legal issues generally dealing with the day-to-day relationships of their citizens. The federal government regulates activities of concern to the nation as a whole, such as the postal system, interstate highways and transportation, national defense, patents, and copyrights. It also has jurisdiction over disputes between citizens of different states and the various states themselves.

The federal system applies to all three branches of government: executive, legislative, and judicial. Both the federal and state governments control the design and operation of their respective jurisdictions. A church in Nebraska is, therefore, subject to Nebraska state law as well as federal law applicable to various aspects of the church's operation.

Stare Decisis

Perhaps the most singularly different aspect of the English system of law after William the Conqueror was the introduction of the rule of *stare decisis*, a Latin term meaning "to abide by, or adhere to, decided cases."[2] This rule distinguishes English and American law from all other legal systems.

Under *stare decisis*, judges decide cases by referring to previous decisions on similar issues. After 1066, the English legal system was revamped in an effort to make it more uniform throughout the country. Judges rode circuit (just as some judges do today). Periodically they met to discuss their cases and decisions. The next round on the circuit, a judge in the southern part of the country might have a case similar to one decided by another judge in the north. The southern judge would look to his colleague's earlier decision for guidance.

---

1. See below for a discussion of common law and the principle of *stare decisis*.
2. *Black's Law Dictionary*, 4th ed., (St. Paul, MN: West Publishing, 1951), p. 1577.

As time passed, the procedure developed even more. Appellate courts began writing their decisions and publishing them in books. These were then distributed to the traveling judges who used them regularly to guide their decisions on the circuit.

In England, the rule is strictly adhered to so that a case many years old can still determine the outcome of a modern case. About the only way the outcome of a case can be changed from a previous decision on like facts is to find some fact that distinguishes the two cases. This can sometimes lead to some truly creative interpretations of the facts.

In the United States, the rule of *stare decisis* applies, but not as strictly as in England. Lower courts are bound by decisions of higher courts, however those higher courts can, and do, overrule former decisions that need to be reconsidered because of changes in society, science, or some other practicality. Overruling prior decisional law, however, is a rare event and is done only when the issue is important and the appellate court feels a need to correct a decision that, while fair when made, could result in an injustice if continued.

Stare decisis plays an important role in U.S. law. It keeps the law consistent and predictable. This is important to lawyers and non-lawyers alike. Lawyers can advise clients and plan legal strategies knowing that the law today will likely predict the law tomorrow. Non-lawyers take comfort in not having to constantly worry whether the rules will change.

By studying a statute, and then reviewing the decisions of appellate courts of the jurisdiction, attorneys can understand how the statute is being interpreted. This allows them to advise clients on the likely outcome of an issue the client brings to the attorney. If there is no statute, we refer to what is often called the common law, that is, decisions on the subject in question. Attorneys keep abreast of the law by studying new appellate court cases that constantly apply previous court opinions to new or slightly different facts.

Though not often discussed in our case law, the principle of *stare decisis* directly affects every case that is decided in this country. It is as imbedded in our legal system as are the basic principles of federalism and the three independent branches of government.

Civil Law in America

This discussion of the principles of state and federal law will not provide any detailed analysis of the separate laws of the fifty states, several territories, possessions, and the District of Columbia. There are, however, general principles of state law that can be described, such as tort, contract, and insurance law. It is important to remember that each state has different, distinct rules applicable to any legal question. Even if several states have similar statutes on a given subject, such as the Uniform Commercial Code[3] (adopted in every state), state courts often interpret them differently. It is important to consult an attorney familiar with a specific state's legislative and decisional law to get an accurate explanation of a state's laws and how its courts interpret them.

Discussion of federal rules or statutes is somewhat easier since, by and large, national statutes and court decisions are applicable nationwide. Nonetheless, as with state law issues, federal law must be interpreted according to the factual situation in question. There are also occasions when the federal courts will look to state law. This discussion can only provide general guidelines. There is no substitute for consultation with an attorney familiar with the law on the area in question.

Civil, or Secular, Law

In canon law we see the terms "civil" and "secular" in reference to laws enacted by civil rather than by ecclesiastical authority. Here we deal only with civil law issues. Civil law deals with an area of law that covers virtually all fields of human interaction other than criminal law. It refers to non-criminal legal principles enacted and enforced by civil authorities.

Criminal and Civil Law

What is the difference between criminal and civil law? In the United States, criminal law encompasses specific acts prohibited by a statute or ordi-

---

3. In the early 1900s, a movement began to develop more uniformity between the states in several areas. This has resulted in the drafting of a number of uniform laws that are then proposed for adoption by the states. Not all states have adopted all of the uniform laws. The Uniform Commercial Code (UCC) is the most notable of the uniform laws and has been adopted by every state.

nance.[4] Punishment for violation of a criminal statute or ordinance is generally limited to imposition of a fine or imprisonment or both. In some jurisdictions, a criminal court may have authority to also impose a requirement of restitution upon a convicted criminal. For example, a drunk driver could be required to spend a term in jail, pay a fine, and pay all or a portion of the hospital bills incurred by the victim he crashed into on the way home from the bar. Criminal fines are paid to the governmental authority (federal, state, or local), not to the injured victim of the crime.

Civil actions involve a wide variety of legal obligations and relationships. In a civil lawsuit, the aggrieved party (generally called the plaintiff) may seek monetary damages to reimburse him or her for the loss caused by the defendant's act. Civil actions can also seek orders of the court requiring a party to: do or refrain from doing something offensive or harmful to someone else; turn over certain property to the plaintiff; remove (evict) the defendant from a location; pay the other party for violating some right, such as a patent, trademark, or even a civil right, such as discrimination. The list of remedies available in a civil action is large and varied. The remedy available in a case will depend upon the right the plaintiff seeks to enforce, or the remedy he or she seeks to obtain. A sentence to jail or prison is not a civil remedy. Jail is exclusively a sanction for violations of the criminal law.

"Civil law" can refer to more than a civil lawsuit. As we have seen, it is often used to distinguish between canon law and systems of law under the jurisdiction of non-ecclesiastical authority. In this context, "civil law" could refer to both civil and criminal legal principles. It is also used to distinguish certain legal remedies or principles from another set of principles referred to as the law of equity or equitable remedies, which are discussed below. Civil law involves virtually all legal relationships and obligations

---

4. Statutes are laws enacted by legislative bodies such as the United States Congress or state legislatures. Ordinances are laws enacted by a municipal or county governing body such as a city council. Legislatures generally derive their authority to enact laws from the constitution that creates them. Smaller governing bodies, such as city councils, have only the authority given them by the statutes that create them. Their power to enact legally-binding rules (ordinances) is narrower and generally limited to issues directly related to the reason for their existence. City and county governments are often referred to as local governments to distinguish them from state and federal governmental authorities.

not specifically under the aegis of the criminal law, though as we will see, there are times the two can converge.

Equitable Remedies

In the early history of the English civil law, the principles of *stare decisis* and strict construction of statutes resulted in what many perceived as unfair or inadequate decisions. For example, if someone stole their neighbor's prize pig, the civil remedy was damages, the monetary value of the pig. But what if the owner wanted his pig back because he had it entered in a county fair and expected it to win (with good reason)? Assume further that this victory at the fair would result in more business and greater wealth for the owner than just the present value of the pig. Or, assume that Sam slandered James, but other than everyone in the village laughing at James, he could prove no monetary loss. If there were no civil remedy, how could one set these situations aright?

As time passed, people with problems that could not be satisfactorily resolved in the civil courts resorted to the church. They would present petitions to their bishop, who would decide the case and order the wrongdoer to take the necessary action to right the wrong. For example, the thief could be ordered to return the pig, and the slanderer could be ordered to publicly retract his slanderous statement. Ultimately, these courts, which were pure courts of equity—that is, they sought to return the balance to the parties' relationship, rather than award damages—came to be called courts of chancery.

Today, our civil justice system has combined the law court system and chancery system into a single system called, simply enough, the civil system. Now a claimant can get his or her case heard in the same court, whether the result sought is damages or an equitable result. For example, in a case of trespass upon one's property that causes damage to the property, and in which the trespasser refuses to stop, the owner may sue for damages (civil law remedy) and for an injunction to prevent future trespasses (equitable remedy).

However, there are some holdovers from the division of the systems. For example, civil cases can be decided by a jury (if the parties agree), but only the judge decides equitable remedies. Thus, in our trespass case, a jury could decide the damages for trespass, but the court would decide whether to award the injunction.

Civil Law System

The American civil law system is, as mentioned, based on the British system. Civil law disputes, whether over personal injury, some other tort, a contract, divorce, or other dispute, begin with one party, the plaintiff, filing a "complaint" with the court. The other party, the defendant, has a specified time in which to file a response, usually called an "answer." Both of these documents state the factual claims of the parties.

There are many steps both sides can take before the case actually goes to trial. Three of the more important of these are:

1. Discovery, in which each side attempts to learn as much about the other side's case as possible. Discovery can include interrogatories (written questions), requests for production of documents and items, requests for admission (asking that the opposing party admit certain statements or facts are true), medical examinations of the plaintiff, views of property, and so on. Usually, there are also depositions (sworn testimony by a witness who responds to questions posed by the attorneys for the parties).

2. Motion practice, in which the parties request rulings by the court on issues such as claims that an opponent has not properly responded to the movant's discovery requests. Other motions can include motions to dismiss some or all of a party's claims on legal grounds; motions designed to clarify issues, limit evidence at trial; or obtain some other benefit for the moving party.

   One very important motion is a motion for summary judgment. This is a special motion in which the movant states that there are no genuine issues of material fact and that the movant should prevail as a matter of law. This tool is often used when one party believes the facts are not in question and the law is heavily on its side.

3. There are often other activities that a client rarely sees, such as searches for and interview of witnesses; laboratory or other scientific or special-

ized testing or evaluation; legal research and preparation of requested jury instructions, as well as extensive preparation of the questions to be asked of each witness at trial.

It is all of these procedures that make a trial so expensive. Among attorneys, it is a general rule of thumb that for every day spent in trial there will be two or three days of preparation.

There can also be considerable post-trial activity. The losing side may appeal to a higher court, forcing the winner to argue the case on appeal. Appeals do not involve retrials; they are considerations of the case based on the legal arguments of the parties about what happened at trial. Even if there is no appeal, the winner may still have to work hard to collect or enforce the judgment.

Administrative Law

Finally, in the twentieth century, the United States developed yet another variation for civil law. This system is called administrative law. It is generally reserved for very specialized areas of law, such as specialized licensing (e.g., attorneys, doctors, real estate agents); immigration and naturalization; and some employment and discrimination cases. In administrative law cases, administrative law judges (as opposed to judges appointed under Article III of the U.S. Constitution, or its state constitution equivalent), who have special experience and training in the field in question, decide the case. There is no jury, and rules applicable to courts of law, such as the Rules of Evidence and many of the Rules of Civil Procedure, are dispensed with. The result is generally speedier and shorter hearings. A disappointed litigant can, of course, appeal an adverse administrative law decision to civil courts.

Alternative Dispute Resolution

A relatively recent development in civil law is called "alternative dispute resolution," or ADR. Although the concept has been around for a long time, its adoption by the courts as a regular part of the civil law system—in some cases it is a prerequisite to a trial—is decidedly new. This is really not a separate branch of civil law; it is an adjunct to it.

There are two basic types of ADR: mediation and arbitration. Mediation involves negotiation between the parties using the services of a third person who assists in the process. This third party is called the mediator, or settlement facilitator. Typically, the parties' attorneys submit summaries of their positions stating their view of the facts and the law. The mediator then meets with the parties and their attorneys to discuss the case. Sometimes, the mediation begins with a plenary session in which each side states its position to the settlement facilitator in the presence of the other party. Sometimes, this step is omitted. In either case, the key to successful mediation is the private sessions the mediator has with each side. In a form of "shuttle diplomacy" the mediator discusses the strengths and weaknesses of the party's position and that of the opposing party. These sessions usually result in the exchange of offers and counter offers. If all works out well, the parties reach a settlement.

The advantage of mediation is that it can occur any time after the dispute arises, but before a trial begins. It is far less expensive than a trial and tends to leave both parties more satisfied than the vagaries of a trial. Perhaps most important, mediation leaves control of a party's case with the party, rather than in the hands of another decision maker—a judge or jury—whose view of the case may not comport with that of either side. A successful mediation also means the end of the case. There will be no appeals since the parties have reached a binding agreement. If mediation fails, however, the case moves toward trial.

Arbitration is another form of ADR. Arbitration is often made mandatory in contracts as a prerequisite to filing suit. One finds this type of clause in many insurance and construction contracts. Of course, the parties can agree to submit to arbitration even if there is no contract requiring it.

Typically, an arbitration agreement calls for the parties to select an arbitrator agreeable to both. Alternatively, some agreements call for three arbitrators with each side choosing one and the two so selected choosing the third.

The arbitrators then hear the case in a sort of "mini-trial." Often cases are limited in the number of witnesses that testify, with the arbitrator(s) reviewing depositions or affidavits of others instead of listening to every witness. The rules of evidence, used extensively in every trial, are either simplified or used only rarely.

In addition to the simplified procedure, arbitration decisions are final. There is no appeal. Unless the losing party can show the decision was based on fraud, or there was evident partiality, corruption, or other misconduct on the arbitrator's part, the decision is final. These grounds[5] are very narrow and difficult to prove. Arbitration has the distinct advantage of being faster, and usually less expensive, than a full trial in a court of law.

The principal difference between mediation and arbitration is that in mediation, the parties themselves decide how to resolve the conflict with the assistance of a third party who has no power to decide the case. In arbitration, the arbitrator(s) (like judges and juries) decide the matter based on the evidence presented to them.

ADR is more and more favored by trial lawyers and clients alike because it is much less expensive than a trial and usually results in a decision more quickly than can be obtained in court.

Conclusion

As we have seen, there are many aspects and nuances to the practice of civil law. The lawyer for the party initiating a suit has to know what legal claims the facts will support and be able to determine the likelihood of success. The attorney must also decide in which forum—federal or state court, or administrative body—the action should be brought. A defending lawyer must analyze the complaint and determine, based upon evidence and the law, whether the case is in the correct forum, what defenses there are, and how best to present the client's case.

Civil law is a complex minefield for the uninitiated. Few cases are simple. The law has a long history, with many nuances. One of the most difficult aspects of practicing law is finding the statutes and decisions that affect a case and then interpreting them in light of the facts.

As stated in the introduction to this section, although attorneys can be expensive, they are far more so if one doesn't consult them early about how to avoid legal pitfalls. Most trial attorneys make more money from people who decide to do it themselves, rather than pay for a lawyer's advice in the first place. It costs more to get out of jams created by this

---

5. The grounds listed are from the Uniform Arbitration Act, one of the uniform laws.

shortsighted view than to get good advice in the first place and avoid the costly consequences of mistakes.

The following chapters will provide an overview of specific areas of the law. They are not intended to be detailed or help you decide how to handle a given case. Rather, the overview is intended to give you a better understanding of areas that can cause problems and of how the law works in some areas.

For Reflection and Discussion

1. Discuss how civil statutes can be affected by court decisions and why.
2. What are the benefits of *stare decisis*? What are its drawbacks?
3. What are the benefits of alternative dispute resolution over lawsuits or trials?

CHAPTER 13

Torts and the Law of Negligence

"Tort" is a catch-all for many different forms of civil action, each with its own rules regarding liability, defenses, and damages. Torts may be intentional or unintentional. Examples of intentional torts include: assault (placing another in reasonable fear of offensive touching or being struck), battery (actually striking another or touching a person in an offensive manner), slander, and trespass on land. Unintentional torts are grouped under the general heading of negligence. Negligence is probably the most common claim made in the civil law arena. It involves failure to meet required standards of care in a wide variety of situations.

Someone is negligent when he or she acts in a way that is below the legal standard of *due care* expected of a *reasonable person* engaged in the same activity. The italicized phrases represent the two basic requirements for everyone in society. To establish a case for negligence, the plaintiff must show that the defendant failed to meet at least one of these standards.

Other elements will apply in a specific case. For example, if Brother Bumble runs a red light and causes an accident with a car driven by Veronica Victim, Bumble is negligent in the way he operated his car because a reasonable driver would stop for a red light. Other examples of negligence could include failure to keep the floors of the parish hall clean of spills so parishioners and other visitors do not slip and fall on a spilled substance; or failure to have child-safe toys and equipment in the parish nursery or playground.

Negligence law breaks an action down into several essential elements. First, there must be a duty owed to the victim. In our car accident case, for example, Brother Bumble's duty is to obey traffic laws, including stopping at red lights. A duty can require one to act or refrain from acting in a certain way. The duty to stop for a red light is an affirmative duty. An example of a situation requiring one to refrain from certain actions is Brother Bumble lighting a cigarette at the gas station while filling the gas tank. He owes the station attendant, Gus Gaseous, and other people there, the duty not to endanger them by creating an explosive situation.

Often, the law specifies duties, for example, traffic laws. However, all citizens have a duty to act reasonably to care for themselves and others, regardless whether any statute on the subject exists. Thus, although a state may set a speed limit of sixty-five miles per hour on a highway, it would not be reasonable to go that fast in a heavy snowstorm or when the road is icy. A resident of a high-rise apartment who drops a book over the balcony, and it falls on poor Veronica Victim's head ten stories below, may not have violated a statute, but has violated the common law duty of due care. The resident is liable to Veronica for negligence. What is reasonable or not in a case is determined by all of the facts.

In deciding whether a person acted reasonably, the court must consider what the person knew, or should have known,[1] of certain facts or conditions. This question may turn on what the person actually knew or could have determined by reasonable inquiry. The duty of reasonable care is also referred to as "ordinary care," the duty to use the same care an ordinarily reasonable person would use in the same or similar circumstances.

Certain professionals, such as doctors and lawyers—and possibly priests, deacons, and religious—are judged by the customary standards in their fields when working in that field. But when performing tasks com-

---

1. The "should have known" issue can be very complex in some cases. A person should know those things that are reasonably apparent. For example, if Sister Educata, principal of St. Learned Elementary School, was aware of a hole in the fence surrounding the school playground, she should know that her young students might crawl through the hole and get injured in traffic on nearby Busy Street.

mon to everyone, such as driving a car, they are subject to the same reasonable person test. The reasonable person test, or ordinary care test, applies to everyone in the common activities of daily life.

Second, negligence law requires that the duty owed be breached, that is, that we fail to meet the requisite standard of care. This requirement may seem obvious, but it is an important issue in some cases. For example, in our red light case, if Sister Share had lent her car to Brother Bumble, she would not be liable for running the red light, even if it was her car that was in the accident.[2]

The third requirement of negligence law is that there be a causal connection between the breach of duty and the injury inflicted. In our red light case, let's assume that Brother Bumble ran the light but didn't cause an accident with Veronica; rather, she was injured when a tire on her car blew out and she veered into the stone pillar supporting the front façade of St. Stalwart's Cathedral. We know that Brother Bumble had a duty to not run the red light, which he breached, but we also know he didn't cause Veronica's injury. Veronica, then, has no cause of action against Bumble because even though he was negligent, his negligence didn't cause any injury. This time, Brother Bumble was lucky.

The last element of a negligence action is damages. Once a plaintiff establishes the first three elements (duty, breach, and causal connection), damages must be proven. In Veronica's case, this could include reasonable and necessary medical care related to the injuries;[3] lost wages for the time she had to take off work because of her accident-related injuries; cost of repair of the damages to her vehicle; and reasonable compensation for her pain and suffering.[4] Finally, if Veronica could prove that Brother Bumble

---

2. Note that Sister Share may not be entirely off the hook, however. For example, if, when she lent the car to Brother Bumble, she knew he had several traffic tickets for running red lights, or that he didn't know how to drive, she would have breached her duty to not lend her vehicle to someone who posed a danger to himself or others. Her tort in that case would be called negligent entrustment.

3. Only those damages related to the negligence are compensable. For example, if Veronica had a broken arm from the accident, she could recover damages for treating the arm. She could not recover damages from Bumble for the sunburn she received at the tanning salon just before the accident.

4. What is reasonable compensation for pain and suffering is left up to the trier of fact based on the circumstances of the case. There are few, if any, guidelines in this area.

acted maliciously, recklessly, wantonly, or had some other high level of culpable mental state, she could recover punitive damages.[5]

As one can imagine, the law of negligence covers a broad range of activities, virtually every area of human endeavor. Every one, particularly those operating places open to the public, such as churches and schools, must be vigilant in avoiding negligence. Conditions on church grounds or in the buildings that pose a hazard to those entering or using them are all good candidates for a negligence claim.

Assuming the plaintiff can establish all of the requisite elements in his negligence claim, the defendant may still not have to pay all of the damages. Not infrequently, the plaintiff is also negligent to some degree. For example, though Brother Bumble ran the red light, if Bumble's attorney can prove that Veronica Victim was speeding, and her speed was a contributing factor to the accident, he may be able to reduce or eliminate any damage award against Bumble. These defenses are known as contributory negligence and comparative fault.

The term "contributory negligence" generally refers to an old, harsh rule, which stated that if a plaintiff were in any way negligent, and that negligence contributed in any way to the accident, the plaintiff could not recover any damages against the defendant, no matter how negligent the defendant had been. Thus, if the plaintiff were only one percent negligent, she was prevented from recovering damages from a ninety-nine percent negligent defendant. Most states have done away with this strict rule.[6]

The vast majority of states have adopted a much fairer rule known as "comparative fault." Under this doctrine, the finder of fact determines whether plaintiff or defendant was negligent. If both bear responsibility for the accident, the fact finder determines how much each was at fault— that is, compares the fault of the parties. It then expresses the relative fault in terms of percentage.

---

5. Note that attorney's fees are not included in this list. This is because of what is known as the "American rule" (as opposed to the "English rule") which states that absent a statute, appellate court decision, or contract provision allowing the court to award attorney's fees to the prevailing party, each side pays its own attorney. The American rule applies in almost every negligence case and in most other civil suits in the United States.

6. As of 1993, only four states—Alabama, Maryland, North Carolina, and Virginia—retained the contributory negligence doctrine.

There are three types of comparative fault. The minority of comparative fault jurisdictions[7] use the pure comparative negligence doctrine. Under this rule, the injured party recovers a proportion of the damages no matter how negligent he or she was. A modified form of comparative fault is used in most jurisdictions. Under this doctrine, the plaintiff will not recover anything if her negligence was as great as or greater than that of the defendant. Finally, three states[8] use a rule that applies terms to the party's negligence such as "slight," "gross," and "remote." How these terms apply to a given situation depends upon the meaning they have in each state's negligence law.

To see how comparative fault works, assume in the case of *Victim v. Bumble* the fact-finder determines that Veronica's damages amount to $10,000. Assume further that Veronica was determined to have been sixty percent at fault in the accident. In a pure comparative fault state, she would recover only forty percent of her damages, or $4,000. In a modified comparative negligence state, she would recover nothing because her negligence exceeded that of Bumble. In the first example, Bumble's liability is reduced by Victim's sixty percent fault.[9] In the second example, Bumble pays Victim nothing because she was more at fault than he was. In the three "terminology" states, the outcome would depend on how the specific terms are defined and applied to the case under the judge's instructions to the jury.

The very best defense against a negligence claim is common sense prevention, or immediate remediation, of conditions that can pose a hazard. It is fairly easy to avoid dangerous conditions on the premises. One way to do this is the common sense solution of observing the property regularly, looking for hazards. For example, are the floor tiles secure? Is any electric wiring exposed? Do you have any leaks in the kitchens or rest rooms? Are

---

7. Arkansas, Arizona, California, Florida, Kentucky, Louisiana, Michigan, Missouri, Mississippi, New Mexico, New York, Rhode Island, and Washington.

8. Nebraska, South Dakota, and Tennessee.

9. Note that Bumble doesn't get sixty percent of the damages from Victim. He must pay her only forty percent of her damage award. However, if Bumble had counter claimed against Victim for injuries he received, the fact-finder would use the same analysis and award him sixty percent of his damages against Victim. She would then have to pay him that amount while he paid her the forty percent of her damages. Obviously, the parties don't actually trade these funds; there is a set-off between them and the one owing what's left pays that to the other.

there holes in the fences around the children's play area? Are food service areas kept clean? Do you use non-skid wax on your floors? The list can go on and on.

The second easy method of avoiding negligence actions arising out of a condition on the premises is to ask the parish or diocesan expert or insurance company to survey the property and buildings. Insurance companies often have trained inspectors who can look over the buildings and grounds and make recommendations for improving safety. Sometimes, following their recommendations can result in a reduction of the insurance premium.

There are also other common sense methods of avoiding negligence arising from parish activities, such as driving vehicles. Before allowing any parish employee or volunteer to drive a parish vehicle, you should ensure they are licensed for that type of vehicle. With employees and those volunteers who will be regularly driving parish vehicles, you may do well to check their driving record to ensure that they don't have a history of arrests or convictions for bad driving. Certainly, any complaints about an employee's or volunteer's poor driving should be taken seriously and looked into immediately. If your parish has drivers using their own or parish vehicles, it may well be worthwhile to have periodic, mandatory classes on safe driving techniques.[10] If your parish doesn't have enough drivers to hold your own class, consider going in with other pastors or even having the diocese conduct courses for a group of parishes. Another possibility is to conduct the classes for parishioners as well as your employees to ensure you get enough attendance.

Does your parish have a kitchen? Is it cleaned after every use—really cleaned? Do you use cleaning chemicals that are approved for use in kitchens serving the public? Do the kitchen and eating areas meet the community's standards for facilities serving food to the public?[11] Have your kitchen workers passed the required health checks? Are they properly trained in handling, storing, and preparing food? Do they wear caps and

---

10. These classes are often available free of charge or at very low rates from insurance companies and police departments.

11. Standards can cover all sorts of things, such as: non-porous walls, floors, and ceilings; proper drainage; proper food preparation surfaces; adequate ventilation; and so on.

gloves? Have you checked on the sources of your foods? Are they healthy and safe? Food preparation is another area where injuries can occur through simple negligence. Who hasn't read of the food poisoning of an entire parish at the annual parish dinner? This is another area in which training and inspections are inexpensive, but can yield great savings through a little preventive common sense.

Almost all parishes have one or more employees. One issue appropriate for discussion here is a parish's responsibility for the negligent acts of its employees. This issue involves two general areas: the vicarious liability of an employer for the negligent acts of employees, known as the doctrine of *respondeat superior,* and the direct liability of an employer for negligently hiring or training employees.

A claim under *respondeat superior* occurs when an employee negligently harms someone else or their property and that employee was acting in the course and scope of his or her employment. To invoke this doctrine, a plaintiff must show that she was injured; the injury was caused by the negligence of the employee; and that the employee was acting within the course and scope of employment. For example, if Frank Fixit, the parish custodian, accidentally drops a hammer while repairing the rectory roof and it hits Billy Bump on the head, injuring him, Bump would have a direct action against Fixit *and* a *respondeat superior* claim directly against the parish. To prove his claim against the parish, Bump would have to show that he was injured because Fixit was negligent; at the time of the accident, Fixit was employed by the parish as a custodian (course of employment); and Fixit was doing a job that was part of his duties as custodian (scope of employment). If Bump can prove all of these elements, he can generally recover his damages either from Fixit or the parish, or both.[12]

Plaintiffs almost always include employers in lawsuits in which an employee was the negligent actor, if they believe they can prove course and scope of

---

12. Bump will be able to collect the total of his damages only one time. That is, he could not collect once from Fixit and then again from the parish. This rule is referred to as joint and several liability. Each defendant is jointly liable with the others for the total damage award and each can also be held to pay the full award regardless of the ability of any other defendant to pay. In no case, however, can the plaintiff recover more than the total damage award; double recovery is not permitted. Thus, if Fixit has no money to pay the damages, his employer, the parish, could be required to pay the whole amount.

employment. This is because the employer is more likely to have the money (or insurance coverage) to pay the judgment.

Direct liability claims against employers arise out of situations in which the plaintiff claims that the employer breached a duty to exercise due care in hiring, training, supervising, or retaining the employee. For example, if the parish hired Raquel Race to deliver lunches to sick parishioners without checking her driving record (or worse, knowing that she had a bad record), the parish could be liable for negligently hiring her to drive the parish truck. On the other hand, if the parish hired her to be the file clerk without any driving responsibilities, it has no duty to determine her driving history.

The same principles apply with regard to training, supervising, and retaining other employees. If an employee is to be doing a job that requires a special ability or knowledge, the employer has a duty to ensure that the employee receives proper training and is supervised in the performance of his or her duties. Similarly, an employer can be negligent in keeping an employee in a job when the employer knew, or should have known, that the employee posed a danger to himself or others in that job.

The duty to act upon negative information regarding employees poses several serious problems for the parish, and often the diocese. No cases better illustrate these dangers than allegations against priests, or other church employees, that they have molested children. A common theme in these cases is that the abuse was reported and either nothing was done or the offender was merely transferred to another post where he was still in contact with children and continued the same pattern of behavior. In these cases, both the parishes involved and the diocese have exposure to liability for negligently failing to supervise the alleged offender, as well as for not taking immediate steps to prevent future abuse.[13]

Arguments that the supervisory authority could do nothing until the allegation was investigated and verified simply will not wash in today's legal and political environment. Once an allegation that a church employee or volunteer has committed sexual or other abuse against a child (or

---

13. An employer could also face liability when transferring such an employee and failing to advise the new employer of the reason for the transfer.

other vulnerable person),[14] the supervisory authority must take immediate steps to suspend the offender's contact with the allegedly abused group, investigate the facts, and take appropriate action.

The argument that the alleged offender is "innocent until proven guilty" will not support a do-nothing approach. There are several reasons for this: First, there is the overriding question of who is innocent: the alleged offender or the alleged victim(s)? Both are entitled to protection until the allegation is verified or disproved. Second, once the supervisory authority is put on notice of such an allegation, the law imposes a duty to act reasonably to ensure the situation does not recur. Failure to do so is similar to handing the car keys to someone who has admitted he doesn't know how to drive as he climbs out of the smoking ruins of the car he just drove into a school bus. Then there is the practical matter of running the parish or school. Doing so with the alleged offender still in his position is virtually impossible. Finally, one must be concerned about leaving the alleged offender in a situation in which he or she could succumb to further temptation. Even if you think that won't happen, if you take no action, you leave the alleged violator in an untenable position.

Given the volume of statistical data and psychological research indicating that offenders of this type don't usually change their ways with counseling, or even imprisonment, it is sheer folly to expect that counseling would be sufficient to prevent a recurrence. The only reasonable response is to remove the alleged offender from the situation, at least temporarily, until the investigation is complete. In doing so, the alleged offender must not be placed in a situation where he has contact with a group similar to those he has allegedly abused. This placement protects both the alleged offender and his purported targets.

If a thorough, unbiased investigation reveals that the charges were false, the alleged offender could return to his previous work.[15] If the investigation substantiates the allegation, the alleged offender must be disciplined

---

14. Allegations can include abuse other than sex or children, for example, an allegation of physical abuse in punishing a student or in dealing with the elderly.

15. It then becomes a management decision whether the alleged offender, now a victim himself, can realistically resume work in the previous assignment.

appropriately.[16] In cases where the investigation is inconclusive, the offender still should not be returned to any position in which he can have contact with the alleged target group. Once the supervisory authority is on notice of the potential for abuse, it has no excuse for setting up a situation in which the potential for repeated abuse is obvious.

Not every person doing work for the parish and who commits a negligent (or even intentional tort) will cause liability for the church. It is a general rule that an independent contractor is separately liable for his own negligence and that the party that contracted with him cannot be held liable for the independent contractor's negligence.

Concerning the case of the hammer falling on Bill Bump's head: If, instead of using the parish handyman, Frank Fixit, to do the roof repairs, Father Scrupulous, the pastor, had contracted with Ralph's Roofing Company to do the work, Bump could sue Ralph for his injury, but the parish wouldn't be liable because Ralph is an independent contractor.

The tests for whether someone is an independent contractor vary from state to state. The most common test is that, first, the actor is not an employee (on the regular payroll), and second, that the parish (or other hiring entity) does not have control over the work (such as how it is done). If both tests are met, the parish will generally not be liable for any negligence of the independent contractor or its employees.

There are multiple exceptions to the independent contractor rule, however. For example, a parish could be liable for negligently hiring an independent contractor it knows is incompetent, or in requiring the contractor to perform according to specific criteria. Other exceptions include failing to inspect the completed work, and situations in which the parish, as possessor of land, has an independent duty to the public to ensure that the premises are safe. Independent contractor situations are heavily fact-dependent and one cannot assume that just because the pastor has contracted with someone else, he has created an independent contractor situation, which will protect him from liability if the contractor is negligent.

---

16. In many of these cases, the discipline can include criminal charges. The church must, however, also enforce its own discipline, such as forced laicization, prohibiting contact with the victim class in future assignments, requiring counseling, and other treatments. Note that the U.S. Conference of Bishops has developed specific rules in this context, which, although very wise under civil law, are binding under canon law.

One final caution may be in order: While it is understandable that a pastor might want to hire someone from the parish to do a job requiring specialized skill, that is probably a poor reason, especially if it is his only criterion. Parishioners are good people, but like everyone else, they can be better or worse at their lay calling in life than non-parishioners. The pastor should choose carefully and check on their ability before he makes a decision.

As you can see, tort law encompasses a broad variety of acts and claims. Its most common form is an action in negligence. The best defense against such a claim is to exercise reasonable care to prevent accidents. Repair unsafe conditions immediately. Get help in identifying potential dangers and take reasonable steps to ensure that parish or diocesan employees are competent to perform their jobs.

This chapter has not touched on the area of intentional torts such as slander, assault and battery (except for the child abuse issue), and other acts directed at intentionally harming someone or their property. Intentional wrongs are fairly easily identified and, therefore, should be fairly easy to avoid. The purpose of this chapter is to introduce you to general concepts of tort law, particularly negligence law, and to provide an understanding of how negligence law functions.

For Reflection and Discussion

1. Describe the difference between an intentional and unintentional tort.
2. What are some ways a parish can prevent injuries on its premises and thereby avoid lawsuits?
3. What steps should your parish take to screen present and potential employees to prevent claims of negligent hiring and retention?

CHAPTER 14

Contracts

Contracts are an exceptionally common form of human activity. Buying groceries, selling holy cards, and charging your account for office supplies all involve contractual relationships.

Of course, some contracts are far more complex. For example, a contract to build a new church or to purchase new desks for the parish school often extends to many pages of legal jargon ("the small print").

Americans enter into contracts all the time. Many contracts are informal (often referred to as "handshake deals"), while others require volumes of painstaking legal draftsmanship. A poorly drawn contract is an invitation to litigation.

Elements of a Contract

Under United States law, contracts have three basic elements: offer, acceptance, and consideration. These elements are absolutely essential for a binding agreement. While these are basic elements, each has an almost infinite variety of nuances and fact issues that keep lawyers in business.

Before analyzing these three elements and other aspects of contract law, we need to be clear on one very important point: It is sheer folly for people not trained in the law to attempt to draw up a contract for an important deal, thinking they will save the money they would have paid an attorney to do the job. Frequently, these self-help contracts result in greater expense when one of the parties sues, alleging a breach of the contract; a dispute arises as to the meaning of a word or phrase; or when a party claims some provision should be in the contract but was left out, all because the parties were not trained in the art of drafting agreements. Many, many hours and much money can be spent arguing over these and other issues, and how to repair the situation.

Here is a common fact pattern: Bob Buyer wants a secondhand car for his son. He doesn't want anything very expensive and would prefer that it not be the kind of car Bob, Jr., could enter in a local drag race. "I just want something he can safely drive to school and his summer job," he tells Mrs. Buyer.

A coworker, Sam Seller, has a ten-year-old, two-door sedan that appears to be in good shape. Sam has a "for sale" sign in the back window of the car.

"Hey, Sam, how much for the car?" Bob asks that very morning when he gets to work.

"Oh, I'm asking $600," Sam replies. "But I'd be willing to work a deal...for a friend," he adds slyly.

"Six hundred dollars, huh? I don't know, Sam. That's a bit high for what I need." Bob then goes on to explain why he's interested in the car.

After some negotiation, they reach an agreement. Sam says, "OK, Bob, we got a deal. I'll sell you my car. You need till payday to get the money, and I need the car until then because my new wheels won't be ready until the end of the month."

Bob agrees. Both shake hands on the deal and return to work happy.

To determine whether Bob and Sam have a contract, we first need to look for the three elements. Sam has *offered* the car to Bob; Bob has *accepted* the offer. We have the first two elements.

What is the "consideration"? Consideration is defined as "the inducement to contract."[1] It can take a variety of forms. In our example of the Bob and Sam contract, the consideration is their mutual promises to exchange the car for money.

Here is another example: If Sister Educata, our school principal, were to hire Tina Rightangle to teach math at St. Learned School, the considera-

---

1. *Black's Law Dictionary,* 306.

tion to the school would be the promise to teach the class competently and in accordance with school requirements. The consideration to Tina would be her salary and fringe benefits.

Consideration, in other words, is the basis of the bargain. It is what the parties contract for.

Consideration itself has three elements: first, the promisor[2] must suffer some legal detriment, that is, do something he or she is not legally obligated to do (or refrain from doing something he has a legal right to do), such as promise to buy a car. Second, the detriment must induce the promise from the promisor. Third, and conversely, the promise must induce the detriment to the promisor. This last element leads to two additional, important aspects of contract law.

First, the offer and acceptance must be communicated. You cannot agree to buy my house if you don't tell me what you are doing. While this may seem obvious, it is a critical point.

The same applies to acceptance. Let's say Hardseat Church Supply Company sends a "special offer" to Rev. Pious, the pastor, that states,

> We are offering a special price on our newest and most uncomfortable church seat—the Sharp as a Rock—guaranteed to keep your congregation awake and feeling penitential during even the most boring homily. You will automatically receive 400 of these seats if you do not return the enclosed response within ten days. Payment is due one month from delivery.

Rev. Pious is not required to respond. If he puts the "offer" in the circular file, there is no acceptance because none was communicated to Hardseat.

The second aspect is that the acceptance must be intentional. If, for example, Harry Homeowner has a home for sale at 123 West Holly Street,

---

2. In a contract, one or more parties can be the promisor(s) and promisee(s), depending on the facts. In the case of Bob and Sam, both are promisors (one promises to give money, the other to give a car) and both are promisees. A contract may be unilateral, such as when Rev. Studius buys a copy of *The New American Bible* at the local bookstore for cash. The store has *offered* him the book, and he *accepted* by paying for it. Implied in the contract is a promise that the book is what it purports to be. If, when he gets home, Rev. Studius discovers that the clerk mistakenly put a copy of *Lady Chatterly's Lover* in his bag; there has been no consideration, and therefore no contract. Rev. Studious is entitled to either an exchange or his money back.

and Sarah Seeker, thinking it is at 123 East Holy Place, tells him she will buy, there is no acceptance of the offer. In terms of consideration, because they are speaking of two different homes, there is no basis for the bargain.

Attorneys often speak of contracts as being a "meeting of the minds." That is, the offer, acceptance, and consideration are all correctly identified and agreed upon.

Returning to the car deal between Bob Buyer and Sam Seller, we now know that the consideration is the mutual promise to exchange the car for cash. There is a meeting of minds. There is a valid contract. But that may not be the end of the story.

Consider this: Predictably, something goes wrong. On payday, Bob approaches Sam with four crisp one hundred dollar bills in hand and says, "Here's your money, Sam. My boy's really excited. He'll be here at noon to get the car."

Sam says, "Hey, Bob, that's pretty funny. Where's the rest of the dough?"

"Rest of what?" Bob says, flummoxed.

"The rest of the money, you cheapskate. The sale price was $500!"

"$500! We agreed to $400. I'm not paying you another dime. I'll sue first!"

"Go ahead, you skinflint. I'll see you in court!"

With that all too familiar threat, Sam hurls the money back at Bob and returns to his new copy of *Car and Driver* magazine (he's on coffee break, you see).

Assuming Bob does sue Sam for breach of contract, how will he prove his case? It's Bob's word against Sam's. The court could rule either way, based upon whom it believed after hearing the testimony. It could just as easily rule that there was no contract because the parties, either through misunderstanding or failed negotiation, never had a deal in the first place—no meeting of minds.

All of this could have been avoided had Sam and Bob reduced their agreement to writing and each had signed it.

While a simple deal like this does not necessarily need an attorney, you would be astounded at the number of contracts for bigger and more complex transactions people attempt to draft themselves, "because it's cheaper than paying some lawyer." Construction projects, land transactions, and sale and purchase of hundreds of thousands of dollars worth of goods are but a few examples. The more complex the deal, the more opportunities there are for problems and disputes.

Contracts to purchase or sell real property or other expensive items, contracts to construct buildings, for employment, and many other forms of agreement must be carefully drafted. They can be long and complex, or they can be short, but complete. They can involve a variety of statutes, ordinances, rules, and regulations, as well as special provisions desired by the parties. When a contract has provisions that require certain activities (such as milestones for construction or events that trigger a payment), the drafting problems increase.

These are not matters for the non-lawyer.[3] They require understanding of what the parties want—often the result of long and careful negotiation—as well as the multitude of legal issues applicable to the contract. Not only do these contracts need provisions regarding what the parties are to do, but what happens in the event of a breach; what constitutes a breach; how the contract can be amended; how damages for a breach are calculated; and so on. Finally, the drafter of the contract must also know what the law requires about contracts on the subject. This is not the stuff for non-lawyers to draft.

Interpreting Contracts

Written contracts are governed by what are called "rules of construction." That is, attorneys and courts use certain rules in deciding what the parties intended when a dispute arises. The most important rule of contract construction, or interpretation, is that the court must determine what the actual intent of the parties was at the time the contract was made. To do this, the court invokes a second important rule, one non-lawyers understand the least: the court reads the contract as a whole; it doesn't pick and choose one word or phrase over another. Another basic rule of construction is that if the terms used are clear and unambiguous, the regular meaning of the words will be used to interpret the contract. If a contract has a definitions

---

3. Lawyers call non-lawyers "lay persons."

section, defined terms will be interpreted according to the definitions in that section.

There are many other rules courts use to interpret contracts. Here are a few examples: A reasonable interpretation of a contract is favored. That is, if one side argues for an interpretation of an ambiguous term that is not reasonable in light of the purpose of the contract and the document as a whole, the court will not accept that side's position.

Any ambiguity in a contract is to be construed against the party that drafted the document. Courts take the position that the drafter of the document has the greatest knowledge of what is in it, and the greatest control. Therefore, if there is an ambiguous term, the courts say, the party responsible for drafting it is the one that should suffer the consequences of the error.

This latter rule is especially true where contracts are drafted and offered on a "take it or leave it" basis. For example, when the insurance agent comes calling with a wonderful new life insurance policy, or hands you the liability policy for your new parish hall, you don't get to negotiate very much about the terms. The company has drafted the policy and will not agree to change it just to make you feel better. This type of contract is referred to as a "contract of adhesion." Courts will look at such documents carefully to ensure they are fair. Many courts have strong precedent and policy construing such contracts against the drafter.

Finally, courts indulge in the presumption that each party has read the contract before signing it. While this is certainly not always true, a party that signs the agreement can be bound by what it says, even if he or she did not take the time to read it. Courts have little patience with the defense of "Oh, I didn't know *that* was in there!"

Evidence

On the other hand, if a provision is vague or ambiguous, the courts may allow extrinsic evidence to help explain the provision. This is referred to as the "parol evidence rule." Parol evidence is generally testimony that helps explain the parties' intent or understanding of a term. It cannot, however, be used to change the terms of the contract.

Statute of Frauds

In the late Middle Ages, English courts had great difficulty with disputes (many of them fraudulent) over contracts dealing with the conveyance of land or contracts that extended over long periods of time. The courts had, by this time, long recognized oral promises as enforceable.[4] However, several significant problems were becoming increasingly frequent: poor memory, or worse, perjury.

In 1667, the English Parliament enacted one of the most significant statutes in the history of the common law: the Statute of Frauds.[5] The statute exists in one form or another in every state in both decisional and statutory law. While the original Statute of Frauds covered a multitude of evils, two of them retain special significance today. Contracts for the sale of real estate must be in writing, as must contracts that will take more than a year to perform. There are variations between states on the statute and in some cases a law may require that the contract be in writing, even if it will be performed in less than a year. For example, under the Uniform Commercial Code,[6] transactions involving a specified amount, or more, must be in writing.

Warranties

Warranties are special provisions in contracts governing what happens when a product fails to live up to expectations or promises regarding quality or quantity. There are generally two kinds of warranty: express and implied. As the terms suggest, express warranties are specifically set forth in the contract. Implied warranties exist by virtue of court decree or statute. Implied warranties apply to a contract, even if they are not set forth in the document. Examples of implied warranties are: good faith and fair dealing

---

4. This had been a matter of necessity since few people of the time could read or write.

5. Its full name is "An Act for the Prevention of Fraud and Perjuries."

6. The Uniform Commercial Code (UCC) is a model statute adopted in all the states. The UCC has common provisions that are supposed to be interpreted identically everywhere. Its provisions apply to many business transactions, but do not cover real estate matters. In practice, however, many states introduced some variations in the statute when they adopted it and each state's courts interpret the UCC slightly differently because of their own common law and efforts to conform the code to a state's other laws on commercial matters. Generally, however, the UCC is regarded as sufficiently uniform that it fosters trade between the states well.

between the parties to the contract, fitness for a particular purpose,[7] and merchantability.[8]

Warranties can be disclaimed. This is true of express as well as implied warranties. The language used must be clear such as, "as is," "without warranty," or "sold with all faults." To exclude an implied warranty of merchantability or fitness for a particular purpose, even more specific language is required. Disclaimer of the warranty of fitness for a particular purpose must be in writing and conspicuous. A disclaimer of the warranty of merchantability must include the word "merchantability" and be conspicuous.

Accord and Satisfaction

Despite the best draftsmanship, disputes can arise over contracts. Often these disputes are resolved without legal action. One means is negotiation. Other ways to resolve disputes are mediation or arbitration, which were discussed in Chapter 12.

Another means of resolving contract disputes can occur under limited circumstances, accord, and satisfaction. This is essentially a renegotiation of the contract. For example, in our car contract between Bob Buyer and Sam Seller, if Sam should decide he really doesn't want to be bad friends with Bob, he might approach him and say, "Look, Bob, I've thought it over. It's not worth it. How about we split the difference? You give me $450, and I'll let you have the car."

Bob thinks it over and says, "Oh, all right. I'd rather not lose a friend over this deal. Here's your $450."

---

7. UCC §2–315. Where the seller has reason to know that the buyer plans to use the goods purchased for a particular purpose, and the buyer is relying on the seller's knowledge and skill to sell the proper product, there is an implied warranty that the goods will be fit for the purpose for which they are purchased. For example, if I ask the shoe salesman for a pair of shoes, I am buying them for general purposes, not a particular purpose. On the other hand, if I tell the salesman that I want mountain climbing boots and need some advice on which ones to get, there is an implied warranty that the boots he recommends will be fit for the particular purpose of mountain climbing.

8. UCC §2–314. When you buy goods from a merchant who normally sells those goods, e.g., the grocer, that merchant impliedly warrants that the goods sold "pass in the trade under the contract description" and "are fit for the ordinary purposes for which such goods are used." Thus the groceries you buy at the local Sac 'em & Eat 'em store are impliedly warranted to be what the label says and safely edible.

"And here's the title to the car. It's in my usual place in the parking lot. By the way, can I get a ride to the dealership where my new wheels are?"

The dispute is now resolved through an accord and satisfaction.

One of the more common examples of accord and satisfaction occurs when one pays a disputed bill by check. Let's say the bill is for $100. The debtor believes she owes only $75. So she sends the creditor a check for that amount and writes "Full and final payment" in the memo portion of the check. If the creditor cashes the check, most courts would hold that it accepted the payment. The parties have reached an accord and satisfaction.

Conclusion

It should be clear by now that contracts can be simple or complex. Contract attorneys make lots of money from clients who, thinking they will save money, decide to draft their own agreements. Then, when a conflict arises, they spend far more money paying attorneys to resolve the problem. This is perhaps the most common example in the legal business of the adage about being "penny wise and pound foolish."

We go through life-making and performing contracts every day, often without thinking about it. Nonetheless, if the subject is important, it is important enough to get the contract properly drafted. If anyone gets insulted that you propose a written contract, drafted by a lawyer, red flags should immediately pop up. It is this type of person that usually causes the biggest problem when there is no document specifying the terms of the agreement. By the same token, if someone hands you a proposed written contract, ask a competent contract lawyer to review it before you sign it. This will help ensure you get a contract that protects you and not just the other party.

For Reflection and Discussion

1. Name and describe the three essential elements of a contract.
2. Why should contracts be in writing?
3. Why is it a mistake to focus on just one word or phrase in a contract?
4. Discuss various rules of construction that courts use to determine what the parties to a contract intended when they signed it.

Suggested Reading

Abbott, Walter M., ed. *The Documents of Vatican II*. New York: Herder and Herder, 1966.

Armstrong, Karen. *The Battle for God*. New York: Ballantine Books, 2001.

Baranowski, Arthur. *Creating Small Faith Communities*. Cincinnati: St. Anthony Messenger Press, 1996.

Bausch, William. *The Pilgrim Church*. Mystic, CT: Twenty-Third Publications, 1989.

Blochlinger, Alex. *The Modern Parish Community*. Trans. Geoffrey Stevens. New York: P.J. Kenedy and Sons, 1965.

Bokenkotter, Thomas. *Dynamic Catholicism*. New York: Doubleday, 1992.

Coriden, James. *The Parish in the Catholic Tradition*. New York: Paulist Press, 1997.

———. *The Rights of Catholics in the Church*. New York: Paulist Press, 2007.

Crosby, Michael. *The Dysfunctional Church*. Notre Dame, IN: Ave Maria Press, 1991.

Davis, Charles, et. al. *The Parish in the Modern World*. London: Sheed and Ward, 1965.

Daas, Ram. *Still Here*. New York: Riverhead Books, 2000.

Dolan, Jay. *The American Catholic Experience*. Garden City, NY: Doubleday, 1985.

———. *In Search of an American Catholicism*. Oxford: University of Oxford Press, 2002.

Dolan, Jay, R. Scott Appleby, Patricia Byrne, and Debra Campbell. *Transforming Parish Ministry*. New York: Crossroad, 1989.

Dulles, Avery. *The Resilient Church*. Garden City, NY: Doubleday, 1977.

Flannery, Austin, O.P. *Vatican Council II*. Northport, NY: Costello Publishing, 1992.

Floristan, Casiano. *The Parish—Eucharistic Community*. Trans. John F. Byrne. Notre Dame, IN: Fides Publishers, 1964.

Foster, John. *Requiem for a Parish*. Westminster, MD: Newman Press, 1962.

Foster, Patricia and Thomas Sweetser. *Transforming the Parish*. Franklin, WI: Sheed and Ward, 1999.

Gibson, David. *The Coming Catholic Church*. San Francisco: HarperCollins, 2004.

Gonzalez, Justo. *The Story of Christianity*. New York: HarperCollins, 1984.

Gryson, Roger. *The Ministry of Women in the Early Church*. Collegeville, MN: Liturgical Press, 1976.

Howe, Ruel L. *The Miracle of Dialogue*. New York: Seabury Press, 1963.

Johnson, Paul. *A History of Christianity*. New York: Atheneum, 1976.

Killian, Sabbas, OFM. *Theological Models for the Parish*. New York: Alba House, 1977.

Kleissler, Thomas, Margo LeBert, and Mary McGuinness. *Small Christian Communities*. New York: Paulist Press, 1991.

Martos, Joseph. *Doors to the Sacred*. Garden City, NY: Doubleday, 1982.

McBrien, Richard. *Catholicism*. San Francisco: HarperCollins, 1994.

McGrath, A.M. *Women and the Church*. Garden City, NY: Image Books, 1976.

McKenna, Kevin E., Lawrence A. DiNardo, and Joseph W. Pokusa, eds. *Church Finance Handbook*. Washington, DC: Canon Law Society of America, 1999.

Miller, Gerald and Wilburn Stancil, eds. *Catholicism at the Millenium*. Kansas City, MO: Rockhurst University Press, 2001.

Muller, James and Charles Kenney. *Keep the Faith, Change the Church*. Emmaus, PA: Rodale, 2004.

Morwood, Michael. *Tomorrow's Catholic*. Mystic, CT: Twenty-Third Publications, 1997.

Rademacher, William J. *Lay Ministry*. Eugene, OR: Wipf and Stock, 2002.

Ramos, Jorge. *No Borders*. New York: HarperCollins, 2002.

———. *The Latino Wave*. New York: HarperCollins, 2004.

Rohlheiser, Ronald. *The Holy Longing*. New York: Doubleday, 1999.

Schillebeeckx, Edward, ed., and Johann-Baptist Metz. *The Right of the Community to a Priest*. New York: Seabury Press, 1980.

Schulteis, Michael, Edward DeBerri, and Peter Henriot. *Our Best Kept Secret*. Washington, DC: Center of Concern, 1987.

Steinfels, Peter. *A People Adrift*. New York: Simon and Schuster, 2003.

Teasdale, Wayne. *Catholicism in Dialogue*. Lanham, MD: Sheed and Ward, 2004

Wallace, Ruth. *They Call Him Pastor: Married Men in Charge of Catholic Parishes*. Mahwah, NJ: Paulist Press, 2003.

Wilkes, Paul. *Excellent Catholic Parishes*. Mahwah, NJ: Paulist Press, 2001.

Winter, Michael. *Blueprint for a Working Church: A Study in New Pastoral Structures*. St. Meinrad, IN: Abbey Press, 1973.

Zech, Charles. *The Parish Management Handbook: A Practical Guide for Pastors, Administrators, and Other Parish Leaders*. Mystic, CT: Twenty-Third Publications, 2003.

Index